Forged In Heat

Book I: Discipline

Joseph D. Randall II

TABLE OF CONTENTS

CHAPTER 1 7
Cold Open 7
CHAPTER 2 14
The Watch 14
CHAPTER 3 19
The Sleep I Never Had 19
CHAPTER 4 25
Aftershocks 25
CHAPTER 5 39
Control 39
CHAPTER 6 51
Nightmares 51
CHAPTER 7 64
Cook School 64
CHAPTER 8 71
Camp Horno 71
CHAPTER 9 78
San Onofre 78
CHAPTER 10 88
Day On, Stay On 88
CHAPTER 11 95
Master Sergeant Overton 95
CHAPTER 12 106

Chief Cook....106
CHAPTER 13....116
WestPac The Ship....116
CHAPTER 14....122
WestPac — The World....122
CHAPTER 15....129
The Courtyard....129
CHAPTER 16....136
Respect vs More....136
CHAPTER 17....143
The Return Across Hawaii....143
CHAPTER 18....151
Return to Horno....151
CHAPTER 19....157
The List....157
CHAPTER 20....166
Pulgas....166
CHAPTER 21....176
Arrival....176
CHAPTER 22....185
The Alarms....185
CHAPTER 23....192
Always Ready....192
CHAPTER 24....200

Food Runs....................200
CHAPTER 25....................208
What Was Left Behind....................208
CHAPTER 26....................215
The Work No One Talks About....................215
CHAPTER 27....................221
The Lesson....................221
CHAPTER 28....................229
Orion....................229
CHAPTER 29....................242
The Accident....................242
CHAPTER 30....................249
Level Three....................249
CHAPTER 31....................261
Back to Pulgas....................261
CHAPTER 32....................270
The Sound Changed....................270
CHAPTER 33....................276
The Long Way Home....................276
EPILOGUE....................286
Contained Fire....................286

PART I: THE BREAK

CHAPTER 1

Cold Open

The desert doesn't have edges.

At night, it disappears into itself. No city lights, no noise, nothing to orient you. Just sky stretching in every direction, wider than anything I had ever known. The darkness out there was not the darkness of a city block or a room with the lights off. It was total. Complete. The kind of darkness that makes you understand, without being told, that you are very small and the universe is very large and neither of those facts is going to change for your benefit.

I lay in the sand, not thinking, not planning. Just looking.

The heat had finally let go. During the day it pressed down on everything, relentless and indifferent, bending the air above the sand into waves that made distance impossible to read. It distorted judgment. It stripped everything down to what was essential. Water. Shade. Attention. Everything else burned away. You stopped carrying anything unnecessary, including thoughts. The desert had a way of editing you whether you wanted to be edited or not.

But at night it released its grip just enough to remind you that relief was still possible.

The sand cooled. Sound carried farther. The sky opened fully.

And the stars did not decorate the darkness.

They overwhelmed it.

Out there, under a sky untouched by city light, the universe didn't feel distant. It felt present. Massive. Unmoved by what was happening on the ground below it. You stopped pretending your concerns mattered the way you once thought they did. Rank dissolved into perspective. Whatever you had been worried about before the desert seemed smaller than it had any right to be.

That perspective changes you.

I had learned to read people the way I read terrain by then. Who moved with economy and who wasted motion. Who watched the horizon and who stared at the ground. Who you could trust when things went sideways and who would hesitate at exactly the wrong moment. Trust didn't form through conversation out there. It formed through consistency. Through watching someone do what they said they would do, again and again, until their word meant something you could stake your life on.

The sand teaches that.

Footprints don't lie. Disturbances show patterns. Wind erases mistakes slowly, not instantly. You learn patience because impatience gets people killed.

When things went quiet, they went truly quiet. Not peaceful. Intentional. Silence meant listening. Stillness meant watching. Calm was never passive out there. It was active awareness. The kind that requires everything you have and gives nothing back except survival.

That kind of calm stays with you long after the desert is behind you.

I was lying in the sand, looking up, not yet knowing what I was looking for, when I saw it.

A pattern.

Not scattered like everything else above it. Not random. Structured.

Three stars. Perfectly aligned. Cutting clean across the darkness like something had been placed there deliberately, with intention, with precision. While the rest of the sky spread out in all directions, vast and complicated and beyond any single mind to hold, these three held still. They didn't drift. They didn't blur. They simply were.

It kept appearing, no matter where I looked.

Orion.

At the time, I didn't know the name. I didn't know the mythology. I didn't know anything about constellations or star maps or what cultures across thousands of years of human history had seen when they looked at the same sky. I hadn't memorized it from a book. I hadn't been told to look for it. No one pointed it out.

It appeared because everything else had fallen away.

I just knew it was there.

Consistent.

Unmoving in a place where everything else felt uncertain.

And that mattered.

Because nothing else did.

The desert removes illusion efficiently. It has no patience for anything that isn't true. Ego doesn't survive long when everyone sweats the same and bleeds the same and the sand treats rank with complete indifference. Out there you find out quickly what you are actually made of, not what you believed you were made of before the pressure arrived.

I had been stripped down to something essential.

And in that stripped-down state, looking up at a sky I had no framework to understand, something shifted.

I wasn't searching for God. I wasn't in a place of prayer or ritual or any of the structures I had been taught to associate with that kind of encounter. I was a young Marine lying in the sand in the middle of a war zone, running on insufficient sleep, trained for violence, surrounded by uncertainty on every side.

But Orion was there.

Fixed. Steady. Disciplined. Present in a way that nothing else around me was.

And I felt, for the first time since the desert had swallowed us whole, that I was not alone.

Not in the sentimental way. Not in the way people use that phrase to soften hard moments. I mean it in the directest possible sense. Looking up at those three stars in formation, something in me recognized that the order I was seeing was not accidental. That the structure above me was not random. That there was a mind behind what I was looking at, a presence behind the pattern, something that had built this and was still, in some way I had no words for yet, attending to it.

To me.

In the sand. In the war. In the dark.

That changed thing.

I didn't announce it. I didn't talk about it. In the Marines you don't walk up to the man next to you and tell him you just had a spiritual experience staring at a constellation. That is not how that environment works. But something had been installed in me quietly, in the way the most important things always seem to arrive. Not with ceremony. Not with noise. With a stillness that you only recognize later as the moment something fundamental shifted.

Orion didn't promise safety. It never made that offer.

It promised orientation.

It was always there when I looked up. Rising. Setting. Reappearing night after night regardless of what had happened during the day. Regardless of what we had seen or done or survived. The belt would cut clean across the darkness again and the message was always the same:

Structure exists beyond the chaos on the ground.

Order doesn't have to be invented. It already is.

You just have to be stripped down enough to see it.

As the weeks stacked and the nights stretched longer, Orion became something I measured myself against. Not a superstition. Not a ritual. A reference point. Something that stayed fixed when everything else was in motion. In an environment where nothing could be trusted to remain the same from one hour to the next, where plans dissolved and orders changed and the ground itself seemed to shift, I would look up and find those three stars exactly where they had been the night before and the night before that.

Reliance. Not belief.

Belief can be shaken.

Reliance keeps you steady.

I didn't have language for what was happening to me then. I was too young, too inside the experience, too occupied with immediate survival to understand that I was being shaped by something larger than the war. That the desert was not just testing what I had already built. It was building something new.

Not toughness.

Not fearlessness.

Something quieter. Something that would take years to fully surface.

An internal alignment between pressure and purpose. Between knowing when to move and knowing when to hold. Between the discipline the Corps had installed and something older and quieter underneath it that Orion seemed to speak to directly.

I didn't know then that this would follow me home.

I didn't know that the discovery I was making, lying in the sand, was the beginning of a relationship that would outlast the war by decades. That Orion would become the name I gave to every company I built. Every venture I committed to. Every new mission I accepted. That it would become the cornerstone of my life after the desert, the anchor I kept returning to when everything else shifted.

I didn't know any of that yet.

I only knew that something was there.

Fixed. Present. Watching without judgment.

And that in a place where nothing else held still, that was everything.

The desert didn't make me who I became.

It revealed what would follow me.

The sand taught me how to endure.

The stars taught me how to orient.

And Orion taught me, without a single word, that there was a Maker behind the order I was seeing. That I was not navigating alone. That the same hand that set those three stars in formation, steady and unmistakable above every desert and ocean and battlefield on earth, was the same hand that had placed me here, in this sand, under this sky, at this exact moment in my life.

I didn't have a name for that yet either.

But I held onto it.

The way you hold onto the only thing that doesn't move.

CHAPTER 2

The Watch

The desert was still dark when the watch began.

That was the first thing you learned. Not from instruction. From experience. The sky above Saudi Arabia didn't transition the way skies back home did. There was no gentle dimming, no gradual softening of light into night. Out there the darkness arrived with authority, the same way everything in the desert arrived. Without announcement. Without apology. One moment there was light. The next there wasn't. And you were standing in it, rifle in hand, responsible for everything that moved within your line of sight.

Or didn't move.

That was the part no one told you about before you got there.

The watch was mostly about what didn't move.

Back home, before any of this, discipline had meant doing something. Showing up. Running the miles. Lifting the weight. Following the order. Moving through the obstacle. The version of discipline I had been given before the desert was always kinetic, always forward, always about action and execution and output. You proved discipline by what you produced. By what you completed. By how fast and how cleanly you moved through whatever stood in front of you.

The desert rewrote that.

Discipline doesn't begin in action.

It begins in stillness.

The watch taught me that. Not as a concept I read somewhere or a lesson a sergeant delivered in formation. It came through the body, the way real understanding always does. Through hours of standing in darkness with nothing to do except be present. Through the particular kind of pressure that builds when you are responsible for safety but have no threat to address. Through learning, slowly and without ceremony, that staying alert when nothing is happening is harder than reacting when something is.

Anyone can react. Reaction is instinct. Reaction is fast and loud and automatic. The body knows how to react. It has known since before you could walk. Threat arrives, the system floods, the body moves. You don't choose that. It chooses itself.

But attention is different.

Attention is a choice you make again and again, in the silence between events, when nothing is asking for it. When the ground is quiet and the sky is still and the only thing demanding your focus is the discipline to stay focused. To not drift. To not let the mind wander into the past or the future or the comfortable numbness that fills the space when there is nothing immediate to address.

That is what the watch required.

Not action. Presence.

I would stand in the dark, eyes moving across the landscape in the pattern I had been trained to use. Near to far. Left to right. Slow. Methodical. Not searching for anything specific. Searching for deviation. For the thing that didn't belong. For the shape that broke the line. For the silence that was too complete, because silence that is too complete usually means something is being held inside it.

Hours would pass.

Nothing would happen.

And I would have to keep watching as though something might.

That is harder than it sounds. The human mind is not built for sustained, empty vigilance. It wants input. It wants problems to solve and patterns to complete and things to respond to. When you give it nothing to work with, it starts generating its own material. Memories surface. Thoughts arrive uninvited. The body gets restless. Fatigue settles in at the edges and starts pressing inward, patient and quiet, testing how long you can hold the line.

You hold the line.

Not because you feel like it. Not because it's comfortable. Because that is what you are there to do and someone else is sleeping behind you and trusting you with their life in the most literal sense possible. That trust is not abstract. It has a face. It has a name. And you do not dishonor it.

So you stay.

And in the staying, something begins to build.

Not skill, exactly. Something underneath skill. A quality of attention that starts to feel different from ordinary wakefulness. A sharpness that isn't about effort but about alignment. The mind stops fighting the stillness and starts moving with it. The ears begin to separate sounds the way a trained musician separates instruments in a chord. Wind from footstep. Animal from mechanism. Distance from proximity. The darkness stops being an absence and starts being a texture, full of information if you are patient enough and quiet enough to receive it.

The watch wasn't about doing something.

It was about attention.

About standing in a position where your responsibility wasn't movement. It was awareness.

And that's harder than people think.

But it changes you.

The discipline of stillness is different from the discipline of action. Action gives you something to measure. You ran the miles or you didn't. You hit the target or you didn't. You completed the task or you didn't. The results are visible. They confirm that the discipline was real and the effort was sufficient.

Stillness gives you nothing to measure.

You stood in the dark for four hours and remained alert and nothing happened and no one saw it and nothing was recorded and no one will ever know whether you drifted or held. Except you. And the quality of the attention you brought to those four hours will show up later, in ways you won't be able to directly trace, as the person you are becoming. As the instincts that sharpen or dull. As the reactions that are fast and accurate or slow and imprecise. As the leader who sees what others miss or the one who only sees what announces itself.

The watch was not glamorous.

It was not the part of service that anyone would put in a story told at a bar or recount at a reunion. There were no medals for staying awake in the dark and watching nothing happen. No one would ever ask you about it or understand what it cost if you told them.

But it was foundational.

Every kitchen I would later run, I ran with that quality of attention. Every team I built, I built with that standard underneath it. The ability to be fully present before anything demands your presence. The willingness to pay attention to the quiet before the noise arrives. To see what is developing before it becomes a problem. To hold the line when holding the line is invisible and unrewarded and the only reason to do it is because it is right and necessary and someone else is counting on you whether they know it or not.

That started in the desert.

In the dark.

Standing still.

Learning to see without reacting.

Learning to be present when nothing is happening.

Learning that discipline, real discipline, doesn't announce itself.

It shows up in the silence between events.

And stays.

unmistakable above every desert and ocean and battlefield on earth, was the same hand that had placed me here, in this sand, under this sky, at this exact moment in my life.

I didn't have a name for that yet either.

But I held onto it.

The way you hold onto the only thing that doesn't move.

CHAPTER 3

The Sleep I Never Had

Nobody tells you about the sleep.

They tell you about the training. They tell you about the heat and the weight of the pack and the miles and the discipline required to keep moving when your body has already decided it is done. They tell you about combat, or the version of combat that can be conveyed in language, which is never the full version. They give you manuals and field exercises and scenarios designed to simulate what it will feel like when it is real.

Nobody tells you what it does to your sleep.

Not because they are withholding. Because most of them don't have language for it either. It happens gradually, quietly, in the way the most permanent changes always happen. Not as an event you can point to and say that was when everything shifted. More like a tide that goes out so slowly you don't notice until one day you look up and the shore looks completely different from how it looked before.

Sleep changed before I ever understood why.

In the beginning, out in the desert, it was practical. You slept when you could, not when it was scheduled, not when your body asked for it, not when conditions were comfortable, because conditions were never comfortable and the schedule was never yours to set. You slept in the gaps. In the back of vehicles. On the ground. In full kit. Weapons within reach, always. You learned to drop into unconsciousness like a controlled fall, fast and deliberate, because the window might be short and the next one might not come for a long time.

That was the first adjustment.

The second was quieter and more permanent.

You stop going all the way under.

It happens without you deciding it. Some part of the nervous system, some deep animal layer that operates below conscious thought, begins to reorganize itself around the new reality. The new reality is this: the environment is not safe. The environment will never be safe in the way sleep requires. True sleep, the deep restorative kind, requires a surrender that the desert does not permit. You cannot fully release when release means vulnerability. You cannot power down completely when complete shutdown could mean you don't wake up at all.

So, the system finds a compromise.

You rest. You do not sleep.

You hover just above it.

Somewhere between being asleep and being ready to move.

That line between alert and asleep, which had once felt like a clear threshold, a door you passed through and closed behind you, begins to thin. Then it begins to disappear. You find yourself on both sides of it simultaneously, resting but tracking, still but listening, eyes closed but some essential awareness still running in the background like a system that cannot be fully shut down because it has been reconfigured to believe that shutdown is death.

In the desert the sounds were specific. Wind across sand has a particular texture. The movement of equipment has a particular weight. Human footsteps at distance sound different from animal movement and different again from mechanical vibration. You learned the vocabulary of the environment without anyone teaching it to you formally, the way you learn any language when survival depends on fluency. Your ears began sorting information in your sleep that your waking mind would have had to consciously process. The body was building a new operating system while you thought you were just trying to get some rest.

Something in the back of your mind keeps running.

Stay ready.

Not as a command you give yourself. Not as a decision you make each night before closing your eyes. As a state that installs itself so deeply that it stops feeling like a state and starts feeling like who you are. You don't choose to be ready. You are ready. Readiness becomes the default condition, and everything else, relaxation, ease, the kind of unguarded openness that sleep once required, becomes the exception that requires effort to achieve.

The nights in the desert had their own rhythm.

You would lie down in whatever space was available. The sand still held the heat of the day in a way that pressed up through your body from below while the night air cooled from above. You found the position that kept your weapon accessible. You closed your eyes. And the process that was supposed to be rest would begin, except it was less like rest and more like a controlled dimming. The volume turned down but never off. The scanning slowed but never stopped.

Four hours was enough.

Four hours was always enough, because four hours was what the situation allowed and the body had recalibrated to function within those parameters the way a machine recalibrates to run on a different power source. You adapted. You adapted completely. And the adaptation that felt like practicality, like the kind of tough pragmatic adjustment that the Corps trained you to make, was also something else.

It was rewiring.

The body was learning a new relationship with rest. With vulnerability. With the kind of trust that sleep requires, the trust that the world will still be there and still be safe when you open your eyes, the trust that nothing will arrive in the dark to take what the darkness always seems to threaten. That trust was being replaced by something harder and more reliable and far less restful.

Vigilance.

Not the vigilance of the watch, which was chosen and bounded by time and relieved by the next man in rotation. This was different. This was vigilance that had moved inside. That had stopped being a posture you adopted and become a condition you lived in. The watch had a beginning and an end. This had no end that anyone told you about. It simply continued, night after night, the body holding its position even in sleep, standing guard over something that could not be named but could not be left unguarded.

You rested.

You did not recover.

There is a difference between those two things that I would not understand for years. Recovery requires surrender and the war had made surrender feel indistinguishable from defeat. Rest was what you could manage inside the parameters of readiness. Recovery was something that happened to people who were safe, and safety had stopped feeling like a state that applied to you.

So, you adapted.

You became someone who could function on fragments. Who could drop into a light suspended state and emerge from it quickly and cleanly, ready within seconds, without the slow fog of waking that other people complained about. You became someone whose body treated every night like a continuation of the mission rather than a pause from it.

That felt like strength at the time.

It felt like the Corps had built you correctly. Like the training had worked. Like you were exactly the kind of Marine the situation required. Hard. Reliable. Consistently ready regardless of conditions.

What you didn't know yet was that the adaptation had no off switch.

That what the desert installed would not uninstall when the desert was behind you.

That the body, once it learns a new way of moving through the world, does not easily forget.

That four hours would feel like enough for a very long time after it stopped being necessary.

That staying ready would continue long after there was anything left to stay ready for.

The sleep I never had in the desert was the first thing the war took.

It was not the last.

But it was the beginning of understanding that some things, once changed, do not simply change back. That the body keeps its own account of what it has been asked to endure. That the tab runs whether you are paying attention to it or not.

I was not paying attention yet.

I was just trying to function.

And for now, hovering just above sleep, the back of my mind still running its quiet unending directive, that was enough.

Stay ready.

CHAPTER 4

Aftershocks

Before I could name it, I felt it.

That is always how it begins. Not with understanding. Not with diagnosis or language or the kind of clarity that lets you point to something and say that is what is happening to me. It begins in the body, in the place below words, in the part of you that registers truth before the mind has organized itself enough to receive it. The body knows first. The mind catches up later, if it catches up at all.

I didn't recognize it as war at the time.

I thought it was adjustment.

I had been through enough transitions to know that moving between environments takes time. You don't walk out of one world and into another and expect the seams to align perfectly. There is always a period of recalibration. Of figuring out what the new rules are and how you fit inside them. I had done it before. I could do it again. This was just the same process at a larger scale.

That is what I told myself.

I was wrong.

What I was experiencing was not adjustment. Adjustment implies a starting point and an ending point, a movement from one stable state toward another. What was happening inside me had no ending point that anyone had mapped. It had no name that anyone in my environment was using. It did not show up as fear, which would have been something I knew how to address. Fear has a shape. Fear has an object. Fear points at something specific and says this is what I am afraid of, and once you know what you are afraid of you can make a plan.

This didn't show up as fear.

It showed up as intensity.

Pressure without a source. Energy without an outlet. A readiness that had nowhere to go because the environment no longer required it but the body had not received that information. The nervous system was still running the program it had been running in the desert, still scanning, still calculating, still holding itself at the elevated threshold that survival had demanded, still waiting for the threat that had organized everything for months and months and had now, without ceremony or acknowledgment, simply stopped arriving.

The system didn't know what to do with that.

So it kept running.

The war had an official end date. Orders were stamped, operations concluded, timelines closed. On paper, it was over. In practice, nothing inside me knew how to stand down. There was no internal signal that said it was safe to exhale, no command that told the nervous system it could finally release. The posture stayed. Shoulders squared. Jaw tight. Eyes moving across every room the way they had moved across every piece of terrain, sorting for the thing that didn't belong, for the deviation in the pattern, for the shape that broke the line.

We were still in the desert.

Still in the sand.

The push through Kuwait had finished but the war hadn't released us yet. The shooting had stopped. The forward momentum slowed. What remained was logistics. We regrouped at base camp, preparing for the long methodical process of sending everyone home. At its height that camp held more than twenty-five thousand Marines. We fed them twice a day. Chow lines still formed. Watches were still posted. Accountability still mattered. Even with the mission technically complete, the machine stayed intact, humming along as if nothing fundamental had changed.

Days blurred together. Heat pressed down on everything. Sand worked its way into seams of boots, into weapons, into skin. Even while packing up, there was no sense of lightness. No feeling of completion. The body stayed braced, as if waiting for the next command to scatter or dig in. You didn't relax because you didn't know how. Relaxing required trust and trust required safety and safety was not something the desert had offered in long enough supply for the body to believe it was real.

That should have been the first warning.

There was no ceremony to mark the transition. No buffer. No decompression between what we had been living and what we were being returned to. One moment everything required vigilance, every sound, every shadow, every horizon line, and the next we were being told to pack up our lives and prepare to return to something called normal. The shift was immediate and absolute, as if a switch had been flipped and the nervous system was expected to comply without resistance.

The body doesn't work that way.

Muscle memory doesn't dissolve on command. Neither does threat awareness. You don't simply step out of a posture that has kept you alive and expect the system to trust that the danger has passed. But that was the expectation. Fold the tents. Break down the bunkers. Dismantle the routines. Move on.

The debrief came next. If it could be called that.

Our commanding officer handed out a thin pamphlet. It fit easily in one hand. No circle. No conversation. No space to ask the questions that were building in every man standing in that formation whether they admitted it to themselves or not. Just a few pages and a brief message delivered without ceremony: not everyone made it home, not everyone would make it home, and not everyone ever gets to go home. Be thankful. Forget what happened. Move on with your life.

That was it.

No language for what we had seen. No acknowledgment of what we carried. No instruction for how to set the pack down.

Just move on.

As we packed up, the tone shifted from reflection to enforcement. New warnings replaced any illusion of closure. If you were caught trying to bring anything back, AK-47s, souvenirs, proof that any of this had happened, you would be pushed to the back of the line. Last Marine out. Last to leave the sand. The message was clear: take nothing with you. Not weapons. Not objects. Not memories.

Then we dismantled everything.

We tore down the base. Collapsed the bunkers. Emptied sandbags we had filled and refilled until the motions were automatic. Policed the area again and again until it felt like we had walked the same ground more times than could be counted.

We erased ourselves.

The place that had held us together was stripped back to nothing, as if we were trying to pretend we had never been there at all. Systematic. Efficient. Emotionally vacant. There was no pause to mark the end of anything. Just a checklist and the next task.

When it was time, we lined up. The processing began. One by one we filtered out of a force of twenty-five thousand, moving toward home. The scale of it was surreal. Thousands of men carrying something unspoken, funneled through a system designed for efficiency, not reckoning. Everyone was quiet in the way people get quiet when there is nothing left to say and everything left to carry.

I don't remember the flight.

Twenty-two hours. Gone.

I don't remember the bus ride from the airport back to Camp Pendleton either. My body followed instructions and stayed upright. My mind refused to participate. It was as if some internal mechanism had disengaged, unwilling to cross the distance all at once.

What I remember is arriving.

Las Pulgas.

The parade deck was full.

Families everywhere. Wives, girlfriends, kids, parents, extended families. Signs held high. Tears. Laughter. Noise. Relief spilling out in every direction. Marines stepped off buses and immediately disappeared into arms that had been waiting months. Names were shouted. Cameras flashed. Futures resumed in real time.

I stepped off the bus too.

There was no one there for me.

No family. No girlfriend. No wife. No familiar face scanning the crowd.

I stood there with my gear at my feet, watching reunions unfold all around me. I noticed how loud it was and how far away I felt from all of it, as if there were a pane of glass between me and the rest of the world. The joy around me felt almost unreal. Like watching a scene through a window, you weren't allowed to open.

I picked up my bags and walked away from the noise.

I walked back to the barracks alone.

That was my welcome home.

April 8, 1991.

Almost immediately the rules loosened. The small disciplines first. No more restrictions on smoking while walking. No rules about chewing gum. Sunglasses with utilities. Salutes softened. The sharp edges of regulation dulled, as if surface relief might somehow resolve what sat underneath.

Then we were given leave.

Immediate leave.

Ninety-five percent of everyone went home.

I didn't.

I couldn't explain it clearly at the time but I knew something wasn't right. I knew I was physically back, my feet on familiar ground, my uniform unchanged, but spiritually something hadn't followed. It felt like my body had crossed an ocean while something essential was still calibrated for survival. I didn't trust myself to step back into a normal environment and pretend everything was fine.

My heart would race without warning. No enemy. No alert. No obvious trigger. Just pressure with nowhere to go.

So, I ran.

At first, it was instinctive. Running burned off the surge. Controlled breathing steadied the system. But it became ritual. Three to five miles at a time. Sometimes three times a day. Morning. Afternoon. Night. Movement was the only thing that made sense. It gave the pressure somewhere to go.

When I wasn't running, I was lifting. Heavy iron. Controlled strain. Different method, same purpose. Containment.

When I wasn't doing either I was calling home.

I would walk down from my room to the payphones, quarters in hand, and call my mama. Call family. Listen to familiar voices, trying to anchor myself to something that existed before all of this. One conversation stays with me. She asked why I wasn't coming home. Why I hadn't taken leave like everyone else.

I told her the truth. The best I could find words for.

I told her I had returned physically but I didn't feel like I was back spiritually.

She went quiet for a moment. Then she told me she understood.

She didn't ask me to explain it further. She didn't push. She just held the line the way she always had, steady and present, and let me know that whenever I was ready, home would be there.

That call held me longer than she probably knew.

As time went on the stories started.

At first they came from somewhere else. Another camp. Another unit. Places just far enough away to keep them abstract. Tragic but distant.

Then they weren't distant anymore.

They were administrative. On our camp. In units we knew.

Marines who had gone home and couldn't process what they found waiting for them. Marriages shattered. Families destroyed. Children caught in the aftermath.

The stories stopped sounding like rumors. They stopped feeling exaggerated. They became names you recognized, faces you had worked next to, men you had trusted to watch your back.

A Marine whose wife had been unfaithful while we were in the sand. He caught her at the club with her new man. Beat them both to death with a tire iron.

Another Marine we knew from before the war. Squared away. No warning signs. He smothered his newborn child.

These weren't unstable men. These weren't outliers. These weren't strangers.

These were Marines we recognized.

Men trained for sustained violence had been sent home with a pamphlet and a handshake. Told to forget. Told to be grateful. Told to move on without tools, without language, without care.

This was the trauma beginning to show itself.

Not on the battlefield. In living rooms.

The realization settled in not as panic, not as shock, but as a heavy suffocating awareness. The system had failed us. Not maliciously. Not intentionally. But completely. We had been trained to endure and then abandoned to figure out what endurance looked like when the mission was gone.

That awareness didn't come all at once. It crept in. Each story added weight. Each silence confirmed what no one wanted to name. Something inside men was breaking and there was no language for it, no permission to slow down, no place to put the weight.

And then my mother went into a coma.

I got the word while I was on base. By then I had eased off the running and shifted fully into lifting weights, pushing heavy iron instead of miles. When the message came everything moved fast.

Emergency leave.

They flew me home. When I arrived at the hospital she had already been unconscious for days. Machines. Tubes. The quiet kind of fear that doesn't announce itself but settles into your bones.

I walked into the room.

She woke up.

Just like that.

Eyes open. Awareness returning. As if she had been waiting.

I stayed home long enough to be present. Long enough to breathe in something familiar. Long enough to remember I was still tethered to life outside the uniform, even if I didn't yet know how to live it.

Then I went back.

Back to the Marine Corps. Back to routine. Back to holding it together.

But we were struggling.

All of us, in different ways.

For me it started showing up physically. During Desert Storm I had gotten sick. For six hours in the field I lost my eyesight completely. No gradual fade. No warning. Just darkness. Then it returned, as abruptly as it left. No clear cause. No follow-up beyond a note in a record that would later matter more than anyone realized at the time.

Then the respiratory infections began.

Tight chest. Burning pressure. Constriction that made every breath feel measured. Recurring. Year after year. The same sickness returning with the same treatment: antibiotics, five hundred milligrams, three times a day, ten days, then release.

Until the next time.

Over thirty years, documented.

Every recurrence pulled me backward. Not as memory. Memory implies distance. This was immediate. The smell. The pressure. The internal bracing. Each episode dropped me back into the same internal space. Hyperalert. Compressed. Waiting.

Doctors treated the symptoms. No one treated the origin.

No one asked what environment my nervous system still believed it was in. No one asked why my body had never fully stood down. The chart said respiratory infection. The chart said antibiotics. The chart said resolved.

The chart was not wrong.

It was just not asking the right question.

Then came the sleep study.

Years later. Long after the desert. Long after the uniform. In a clinical setting, hooked to monitors, observed through a night that was supposed to finally give someone a clear picture of what was happening inside a body that had never fully stood down.

The results came back.

In a given hour, stopping breathing more than thirty times is considered extreme. It signals a system under serious, sustained stress. It means the body is fighting for air in the moments it should be releasing. It means rest, the kind the body is supposed to use for repair and restoration, is being interrupted so frequently that it barely registers as rest at all.

During my study they recorded 122.2 AHI.

One hundred and twenty-two times in a single hour.

Not thirty. Not fifty. Not the number that gets you labeled extreme and sent home with a machine and a follow-up appointment.

One hundred and twenty-two.

The technicians noted it. The doctors documented it. The language used was clinical and careful and thoroughly inadequate for what that number represented when you understood where it came from.

This was not a sleep disorder that arrived randomly.

This was the body's account of decades spent in a state the desert had installed and nothing had ever fully dismantled. Thirty years of the nervous system running at elevated threshold. Thirty years of the body holding its breath, literally, in the hours when it was supposed to finally exhale. Thirty years of the watch continuing long after the watch was over, expressing itself now not through dreams or hypervigilance or respiratory infections but through the most fundamental biological function there is.

Breathing.

The sleep I never had in the desert had not simply followed me home.

It had compounded.

Year after year, night after night, the body keeping its own account with the precision of something that does not forget and does not forgive and does not stop adding to the tab just because you have stopped paying attention to it.

One hundred and twenty-two times in a single hour.

That number is not a medical statistic.

It is the full cost of the silence finally presenting its invoice.

The body replayed what the mind had never been allowed to resolve.

This is how it hides. Not as flashback. As repetition. As the same pattern returning again and again in different forms, each time requiring the same response, each time taking something from you that doesn't fully come back.

Aftershocks don't announce themselves as trauma.

They present as patterns.

As reactions that seem disproportionate until you understand the scale they are responding to is not present anymore. Until you understand that the body is not being irrational. It is being loyal. Loyal to the environment that shaped it. Loyal to the threat it was trained to prepare for. Loyal to the version of the world it learned to survive in, long after that world has formally ended.

The war was over.

The body hadn't gotten the message.

And then the stories stopped being shocking.

They became expected.

That was the moment that cut the deepest. Not fear, not surprise. Recognition.

Terror.

Not the loud kind. Not panic.

The quiet kind.

The kind that settles in your chest when you realize something has gone catastrophically unaddressed. When you understand that what is happening isn't random and it isn't rare.

It's structural.

This is what happens when men are trained to endure but not to come home. When discipline is mistaken for healing. When silence is treated as strength. When a thin pamphlet and a handshake are considered sufficient preparation for re-entering a world that has no framework for what you are carrying.

I was still standing. Still functioning. Still wearing the uniform.

But the pressure was there.

Building quietly.

Waiting for the structure that was holding it to finally run out of walls.

CHAPTER 5

Control

Nobody teaches you control.

Not really. Not the kind that matters. Not the kind that becomes so deeply woven into the fabric of how you move through the world that it stops feeling like a choice and starts feeling like your actual character. That kind of control is not taught. It is installed. By pressure. By repetition. By environments that make absolutely clear, without sentiment or explanation, that the alternative to control is consequences you cannot afford.

The Marine Corps installed it in me the way the desert had installed sleep deprivation. Not as a lesson I received. As a condition I lived in until it became the only condition I knew.

Control did not arrive as an idea I evaluated or debated.

It arrived as instinct.

Already running in the background before I knew to question it. Already trusted before I had tested it deliberately. Already mine in the way that things become yours when you have relied on them long enough that you can no longer imagine who you would be without them.

By the time the war ended, control was not a tactic or a choice. It was posture. It was how my body occupied space. How my attention sorted threat from noise. How my nervous system decided what mattered and what could safely be ignored. It was the operating system underneath everything, running continuously, never fully powering down, organizing my experience of the world into two categories: things that required attention and things that didn't.

There was very little in the second category.

After Desert Storm, nothing inside me loosened. There was no internal ceremony marking the end of vigilance, no clean psychological handoff from survival to rest. Orders ended. The mission ended. The calendar said we were done. My body never received the message. My shoulders stayed squared. My jaw stayed tight. My breathing stayed shallow even in quiet rooms. Even when there was nothing to watch, some part of me was still scanning, still measuring distance, still calculating what might go wrong and what the response would need to be and how fast I would need to move.

I didn't question that posture.

I relied on it.

It had kept me alive when the world made no sense at all. You don't audit the thing that kept you alive. You don't take it apart to see how it works. You keep it exactly as it is, maintained and ready, because the next moment it might be needed is always closer than you think.

Control became the way forward.

Not control in the sense of authority or dominance over other people. Not the kind that announces itself loudly or demands recognition. This was quieter and more interior. It was about containment. About keeping the internal pressure, the pressure that Chapter 4 had started building, from spilling outward into the spaces where it could cause damage to the people around me and to the life I was trying to maintain.

The stories I had heard. The men I had watched detonate. The tire iron. The newborn. The marriages destroyed and the families erased. Those stories were not abstract cautionary tales to me. They were mirrors. I understood, with a clarity that did not require analysis, that nothing separated those men from me except the circumstances that had triggered them. We had all been trained the same way. We had all been sent home with the same pamphlet and the same handshake and the same instruction to move on.

What they had released, I contained.

Control promised safety. Not the kind the desert had withheld, not physical safety, not the guarantee of survival. A different kind. Predictability. The assurance that I would not become the story someone else told. That my name would not appear in the administrative report on someone else's unit. That the thing the war had built inside me would stay inside me, directed and managed and never unleashed on anyone who had not earned it.

That was the promise I made to myself.

I didn't decide to control my life.

I organized it.

Organization felt responsible. Adult. Moral, even. There is a story the culture tells about discipline, that it is virtuous, that it is the mark of a serious and reliable person, that the more tightly you manage yourself the more worthy of trust you become. That story fit perfectly over what was actually happening, which was that I was managing internal pressure by building external structure so tight that nothing could get in and nothing could get out.

The more controlled I became the more functional I appeared.

From the outside everything looked stable. Strong. Squared away. There were no visible cracks. No warning signs that suggested anything underneath required attention. People saw a Marine. They saw discipline and reliability and the kind of steadiness that is rare enough in the world to be genuinely valued. They trusted me with things because I had demonstrated, repeatedly and consistently, that I would not drop them.

Inside, control felt like holding pressure inside a sealed container.

As long as the walls held, nothing leaked. Nothing alarmed anyone. Nothing forced a conversation I was not equipped to have. Silence became proof that the system was working. If nothing was spilling out, then nothing needed to be addressed. That was the logic. It was not entirely wrong. It was just not complete.

The military reinforced that instinct without ever naming it. Hierarchy didn't disappear when combat ended. Structure remained. Schedules. Ranks. Expectations. Consequences. Familiar systems meant fewer unknowns. Fewer unknowns meant less risk. Risk had become the enemy after the war, not because danger was present, but because my body no longer trusted calm. Calm had always preceded something. In the desert, the quiet moments were the ones that required the most attention because quiet was when things shifted without warning.

That association did not dissolve just because the desert was behind me.

Control created distance.

Emotion complicates systems. Emotion introduces variables. Variables slow execution and execution had been the thing between living and not living for long enough that the equation had been permanently installed. So emotion was managed. Not denied outright. Cataloged. Deferred. Set aside. Not with drama, not with visible suppression, just quietly deprioritized because it didn't serve the immediate function. There would be time for it later.

Later became a moving target that never arrived.

I wasn't numb. I want to be precise about that. Numb suggests absence. What I had was not absence. It was focus. Focus so complete and consistent that it functioned like absence from the outside, but from the inside it felt like being entirely present in a very narrow place.

Focus narrows perception. Narrow perception feels calm. Calm feels safe. Safe feels earned.

That narrowing extended into everything. How I spoke. How I moved. How I listened. Conversations became functional. Direct. Efficient. If something didn't have a clear purpose it didn't need airtime. The kitchen rewarded that completely. You don't have long conversations during service. You communicate in shorthand, in commands, in confirmations. Language is compressed to its most essential form because everything else is waste and waste costs time and time costs food and food costs reputation.

Work became the safest place to stand.

Not because it was easy. Because it was structured. Expectations were clear. Outcomes were measurable. Effort translated into results you could see and touch and serve to another person who would either confirm they were good or tell you they weren't. There was no ambiguity in that. No interpretation required. The feedback was immediate and concrete and the correction was immediate and concrete and the whole system operated on a logic I understood in my body the way I had understood the logic of the desert.

You follow the process. You get the result.

Kitchens mirrored that architecture perfectly. Hierarchy, timing, precision, accountability. Orders given. Orders executed. Mistakes corrected immediately. No ambiguity about who was responsible when something went wrong. The kitchen didn't create control in me. It reflected what was already there. It gave it a container that the rest of the world recognized as professional rather than as a symptom.

The kitchen didn't create control.

It reflected it.

Precision became insulation. Mise en place was not just preparation. It was the physical expression of everything I believed about order and safety. When everything was in its place nothing surprised you. Repetition reinforced safety. Clean stations. Clean lines. Clean execution. Each task flowing into the next without interruption. Presence mandatory because presence in a kitchen is not optional. You cannot drift. You cannot disappear into your head while something is on the fire. Your hands have to be where your attention is.

There was real relief in that.

The kitchen required all of me, all the time, in a way that left no room for what I was carrying to surface. It was the most legitimate form of avoidance I had ever found. Legitimate because it produced something. Because the avoidance translated into craft. Because the pressure that had nowhere else to go went into the food and the food was excellent and excellence was recognized and recognition felt, for brief moments, like the thing I had been searching for since the parade deck.

But relief is not release.

And that distinction matters more than almost anything else in this story.

Control doesn't discharge pressure. It redistributes it. It takes the weight from one place and moves it to another. It compresses what cannot be expressed into denser and denser forms, burying it deeper, packing it tighter, trusting that the walls of the container are strong enough to hold indefinitely.

They are not.

As responsibility increased so did the demand to hold everything together. Reliability became identity. Being the one who handled things. The one who absorbed problems before they became visible. The one people trusted not to fail. That role looks like leadership and in many ways it was. It earns respect. It builds teams. It creates environments where people know they can count on someone to be exactly what they say they will be.

It is also heavy in ways that never appear on the outside.

Control requires vigilance. You cannot set it down. You cannot loosen your grip without consequences because the moment you loosen your grip is the moment something slips and something slipping is the beginning of the sequence you have been holding off since April 8, 1991 when you walked alone across a parade deck while everyone else disappeared into arms that had been waiting.

Rest becomes suspicious. Downtime feels unsafe. Stillness invites things you have been outrunning. If you are not actively managing something, something is managing you.

So you stay on.

Always on.

Days compressed into execution loops. Wake up already alert. Move through tasks with precision. Monitor details others missed. Anticipate problems before they surfaced. Fix things quietly so they showed no evidence of having been broken. End the day without visible damage. Repeat.

There was genuine satisfaction in that rhythm. It reduced the number of decisions I had to make. Fewer decisions meant fewer chances to drift into the territory where the things I hadn't processed were waiting. The structure was functional. The structure was real. I built things inside that structure that mattered and that I am proud of and that served people well.

And underneath all of it, quietly, without announcement, the cost was accumulating.

The emotional range narrowed so slowly it was almost imperceptible. Joy flattened. Anger compressed. Sadness quieted until it was barely audible. Everything passed through the filter of function. You become fine. Fine enough to work. Fine enough to show up. Fine enough not to raise concern in anyone who might otherwise have looked closer.

Fine is dangerous because it hides everything.

People stop asking questions when the answer is always fine. Systems stop checking in when nothing appears broken. The less visible the accumulation the more it accumulates because no one is intervening and no one is intervening because there is nothing visible to intervene with.

The body pays the price first.

Always the body.

Sleep stops restoring. It pauses the system but doesn't reset it. Mornings arrive with obligation instead of renewal. Tension becomes baseline. Muscles stay engaged even when there is no task to justify it. The nervous system hums constantly, unable to power down, keeping its watch long after the watch is over because no one has been given permission to stand down.

You forget what relaxed feels like.

Not because it is unavailable. Because you no longer trust it. Because relaxed means open and open means unguarded and unguarded, in the body's memory, means the thing that used to get you killed.

Control isolates without meaning to.

Not socially. I was surrounded by people, by kitchens, by teams, by the constant noise and movement and demand of professional environments. But internally. You do not invite others into a system you pride yourself on managing alone. You do not burden them with the complexity underneath when your entire identity is built on being the person who handles complexity. Conversations stay safe. Surface-level. You become extraordinarily skilled at presence without openness, at being fully in the room while keeping the room's access to you carefully controlled.

That skill looks like maturity from the outside.

From the inside it feels like standing behind glass.

Watching everything. Unreachable by anything.

Deferred things don't disappear.

They accrue interest.

Pressure doesn't announce itself while it's building. It doesn't shout. It whispers. It asks quietly for more. More attention. More vigilance. More effort. More compression. And you give it because control has always worked. It has never failed you. It has gotten you through the desert and through the return and through thc parade deck and through the stories and through the years of recurring infections and through every kitchen and every team and every morning that arrived with obligation instead of renewal.

Control is strongest right before it fails.

I didn't see it as temporary. I saw it as refinement. Growth. The ongoing development of a person who was becoming more capable, more dependable, less vulnerable to the kind of catastrophic unraveling I had watched happen to men I respected. I took pride in how little rattled me. In how steady I appeared. In how rarely I needed anything from anyone.

I didn't recognize that vulnerability hadn't vanished.

It had been stored.

Stored tension becomes rigidity. You stop bending and start holding yourself in a single fixed position because bending feels like the first step toward breaking. Stored emotion becomes pressure. Stored memory waits with the particular patience of something that knows it will eventually be heard.

Control held everything in place.

Including what would eventually demand release.

For a long time, that felt like success.

I was functioning. Advancing. Building something. Maintaining something that looked, by every external measure, exactly as it should. No dramatic collapses. No visible failures. No public unraveling. By the standards of every environment I moved through, control was working exactly as intended.

That's the danger of control.

When it works, it justifies itself.

It convinces you that nothing else is needed. That endurance is the same as healing. That stability is the same as integration. That silence is strength. That the man who never breaks down is the healthy man rather than the man who has built a container strong enough that the breakdown cannot yet be seen.

Control does not ask whether you are whole.

It only asks whether you are operational.

I stayed operational.

The cost accumulated quietly. In the body. In the breath. In the constant readiness that never fully shut off. Control was doing more work than it was designed to do. It was compensating for what had never been processed, for what had never been named, for what the desert had built and the pamphlet had refused to acknowledge and the years had simply added to, layer by layer, the way sand adds to a dune. Slowly. Without drama. Until the shape of it is undeniable to anyone willing to look.

Still, it held.

And as long as it held there was no reason to question it.

The danger wasn't collapse.

The danger was that it was succeeding too well.

That the container was strong enough to hold the pressure far longer than was good for anyone living inside it. That strength and endurance, the very things the Corps had built in me and the desert had refined and the kitchen had given daily purpose, were the same things that would delay the reckoning long past the point where it should have arrived.

For now, control remained the strategy.

The structure. The container. The way forward through a world that had no other framework to offer.

It was enough.

Until it wasn't.

CHAPTER 6

Nightmares

The days had a structure. The nights did not.

That asymmetry was the thing nobody warned you about. During the day there were still formations, still kitchens, still tasks and timelines and people who needed things from you at specific hours. The machinery of service kept moving even after the war officially ended, and as long as the machinery was moving you had somewhere to put yourself. You had a role. You had a function. You had the particular relief that comes from being needed in a way that is concrete and measurable and doesn't leave room for the mind to wander into territory you are not ready to enter.

The days held you together.

The nights were a different country entirely.

The nights came after.

Not immediately. Not while we were still moving, still packing, still dismantling the machinery of war piece by piece, still feeding twenty-five thousand Marines twice a day and standing watch and processing out of a base we had spent months building and one checklist tearing down. As long as there were tasks, schedules, formations, and obligations, the days stayed loud enough to keep everything contained. The body remained busy. The mind stayed occupied. There was no silence long enough for anything buried to surface.

Because buried things require silence.

That is the condition they wait for. Not drama. Not crisis. Not the moments of highest intensity when everything is happening at once and the system is fully engaged and there is no bandwidth for anything beyond the immediate demand. Those moments are the safest, in a way. The most dangerous moments are the quiet ones. The ones that arrive after the task is finished and before the next one begins. The ones at the end of the day when the structure that has been holding everything in place finally steps back and the thing underneath is left standing in the open without anything to hide behind.

Nightmares require stillness.

They require the world to quiet down enough for what has been stored, unprocessed, unnamed, unresolved, to find a voice. And the desert had given me more to store than I had language for. Not just the things I had seen, the burnt vehicles and the bodies and the alarms that gave you seven seconds to decide what to do with your life. Not just the specific moments of impact. The accumulation. The months of sustained vigilance. The sleep that was never fully sleep. The food runs through what used to be front lines. The smell of things that do not leave your memory no matter how efficiently you try to organize the memory away.

All of it had been stored.

And now the nights were very quiet.

At first sleep didn't feel dangerous. It felt thin and incomplete, the way it had always felt in the desert, the hovering half-conscious state that was less like sleeping and more like powering down briefly before rebooting. I would close my eyes and open them again without clear memory of what had happened in between. Some part of me never fully disengaged. Some part stayed half-awake, standing watch the way Chapter 2 had taught me to stand watch, attentive even in the absence of anything to be attentive to.

That felt normal.

It was the only version of sleep I had known for so long that I had stopped recognizing it as unusual.

Then the dreams arrived.

They did not arrive gently or logically. They did not announce themselves. They did not give me time to prepare a response or build a structure around them or apply the same organized containment that had worked on everything else. They arrived the way the worst things always arrive, without warning, in the place where the defenses were lowest, in the hours when the body had finally committed to something that resembled rest.

They were not cinematic reenactments of combat.

I want to be clear about that because it matters. People who have not experienced this expect the nightmares to be replays. They expect you to see, in your sleep, the specific events that traumatized you, projected on the back of your closed eyelids like a film you cannot stop. That is not how it works. Or it was not how it worked for me. The dreams were not about what had happened. They were symbolic. Invasive. Personal in a way that went deeper than specific memory. They bypassed the catalog of events entirely and went straight to meaning. Straight to the things underneath the events. Straight to what the events had done to the person who had lived through them.

I would wake with my heart already racing.

Breath shallow. Muscles tight. The body already in the state that comes after a threat has been assessed and responded to, the elevated ready state that follows action, except there had been no action. I had been asleep. Nothing had happened in the physical world. And yet the body had been somewhere, had done something, had responded to something with the full force of everything it had been trained to do, and the evidence of that was written in every system: elevated heart rate, shallow breathing, muscles engaged, awareness flooding in faster than the conscious mind could organize it.

Fear arrived first.

Then alertness. Fully formed. Immediate.

The body reacted as if something had happened even when the conscious mind could not locate what it was. And that absence of a locatable cause was its own particular kind of disorientation. In the desert when your body went into that state there was always a cause. An alarm. A sound. A movement at the edge of your line of sight. Something you could identify and assess and respond to or stand down from once assessed. The system had a logic. Input, response, evaluation, resolution.

The nightmares broke that logic.

The input was invisible. The response was full and complete. The evaluation found nothing in the physical environment to account for it. And resolution never came because you cannot stand down from a threat you cannot locate.

As the weeks passed the dreams sharpened.

Images repeated. Settings returned. Patterns formed. Something was knocking from the inside and it was not interested in being ignored.

The dreams were not about the battlefield.

They were about violation.

One dream returned again and again. Not always in the same form but always carrying the same weight. I was back in the barracks. Home. Familiar. The place that was supposed to be the safe perimeter, the interior after the exterior had been secured, the inside of the line. Supposedly safe.

There was something on the wall. A poster. Something that stood for belief. For identity. For the moral ground I had been standing on, the thing underneath all the discipline and training and endurance that told me why any of it mattered. Someone attacked it. Not verbally, not with argument or disagreement, but physically. With force. With intent to destroy it.

Something primitive took over.

No hesitation. No negotiation. No pause to evaluate or consider proportionality or what the response would look like to someone watching from outside. Immediate force in defense of something sacred. The response was absolute and certain in a way that nothing in my waking life was absolute and certain anymore.

I woke before resolution every time.

Always before I knew what had happened. Always in the middle of the action, never at the end of it, never with the closure of knowing what the outcome had been or whether the thing on the wall had been defended or destroyed.

The clarity unsettled me more than the violence.

Not the violence itself. The certainty of the response. The absence of doubt. The part of me that had appeared in the dream was not confused or conflicted or calculating. It knew exactly what it was doing and it was doing it without apology and without hesitation and with a completeness of commitment that my waking self, which was very busy managing and containing and organizing and deferring, had lost access to.

The dream did not create that part of me.

It revealed it.

It showed me what was still running underneath the structure. What the control of Chapter 5 was actually containing. Not just pressure and unprocessed memory and the residue of sustained vigilance. Something older and more elemental. The part that the Corps had trained and the desert had refined and the war had activated, the part that responded with absolute force when something it recognized as sacred was threatened, regardless of context or consequence.

That part had not stood down.

It had gone underground.

And it was speaking, the only way it could, in the hours when the structure stepped back and the guards were down and the organized functional performing version of me was finally quiet enough for something else to be heard.

The dreams did not follow a schedule.

Some nights they came back-to-back, relentless and layered, one dissolving into the next before I could fully surface from the first, each one leaving its residue before the next one arrived. Those nights were exhausting in a way that sleep was supposed to prevent. I would wake more depleted than when I had closed my eyes, as if the night had extracted something rather than restored it.

Other nights they disappeared entirely.

Those nights were almost worse.

Because the absence created hope and hope, in this context, was a liability. I would lie down and sleep would come and the night would pass and I would wake in the morning in something that felt like the normal version of tired rather than the particular exhaustion of a night spent somewhere my body would not tell my mind about. And I would think, quietly, carefully, not wanting to fully form the thought in case the thought itself was what broke the spell: maybe it is finished. Maybe whatever needed to be expressed has been expressed. Maybe the system has worked through it and I can move forward now without this particular weight.

That hope never lasted.

When the dreams returned they were sharper than before. More precise. As if the system had been using the quiet nights not as rest but as refinement. As if what was trying to communicate itself had taken the pause to figure out a more exact way to say what it needed to say, and returned with the message clarified, the imagery more targeted, the emotional impact more direct.

Patient. Methodical. Unwilling to be outrun.

During these cycles the days began to change.

This was the part that frightened me more than the dreams themselves. The nights were their own contained world that I had accepted, reluctantly but practically, as a condition I was managing. What I had not accounted for was the way the nights would begin reshaping the days. The way the residue from one would transfer into the other until the boundary between them started to blur.

I noticed how alert I was to tone.

Not just to words, to the tone beneath the words. To the quality of someone's attention when they spoke to me. To the micro-shifts in posture and expression that preceded mood changes. To the particular register of silence that meant something was being held back versus the register that meant nothing was there. I had always been attentive. The watch had made me attentive. But this was different. This was attentive tipping toward surveillance. Toward a level of environmental monitoring that was exhausting to maintain and impossible to switch off.

Rooms felt different.

I cannot explain this in a way that sounds rational because it was not rational. It was somatic. The body's assessment of space, its reading of threat and safety in a given environment, had been recalibrated so completely by the desert that rooms which should have felt neutral felt loaded. The position of a door. The number of people between me and the exit. The sightline from where I was sitting to where movement was most likely to originate. These were not thoughts I was choosing to have. They were the automatic output of a system still running the desert's operating instructions in a world that had moved on.

Silence felt loaded.

Not the silence of Chapter 2, the intentional watchful silence that was presence made active. A different kind. The kind that felt like it was about to break in a way you could not predict and could not prepare for because the threat, if there was a threat, was not visible and not locatable and not addressable with anything in your current inventory.

Authority felt fragile.

I trusted fewer people with fewer details.

The nights were shaping the days even when I pretended they were separate. Even when I maintained the structure and showed up and executed and was fine, fine, always fine, the residue was there. In the narrowed patience. In the compressed tolerance for anything that felt like a wasted motion or an unnecessary variable. In the distance that had grown between the version of me that was present in every room and the version of me that was actually accessible to anyone in it.

I did not talk about the dreams.

Not because I was ashamed, though shame was present. Because there was no container for what I would have needed to say. Dreams were treated in that environment as noise. As imagination. As weakness at worst and irrelevance at best. There was no framework for symbolic threat. No language for moral injury. No space in the culture of discipline and forward movement for someone to sit down and say the nights are doing something to me that I do not have words for and I need help finding the words.

So, I did what I had always done.

I contained them.

Containment works.

Until it doesn't.

Sleep became territory I had to manage strategically rather than enter naturally. I learned to go to bed exhausted. Exhausted enough that the transition from waking to sleep would be fast, too fast for images to form in the hovering space between them. Less hovering meant less opportunity for whatever was waiting in the threshold to get a foothold.

When exhaustion worked it felt like a victory. Like I had outmaneuvered something that was trying to get to me. Like the strategy was sound and the system was holding and I was still, in this as in everything else, the one in control.

When it didn't work the nights reminded me that control had limits.

That there were things it could not organize away.

That the pressure it was redistributing had to go somewhere eventually and the dreams had found the place where eventually arrived.

The dreams were not flashbacks. They were not replays of specific events. They were questions dressed as threat. Dressed in the imagery and emotional register of danger because that was the only language the part of me asking them knew how to speak.

What happens when belief is attacked?

What happens when safety is violated from inside the perimeter?

What happens when the rules that were supposed to hold everything together dissolve?

What happens when the system fails the people who trusted it?

I didn't have answers.

I only had endurance.

And endurance, as Chapters 4 and 5 had already demonstrated and this chapter was confirming, is not the same as healing. It is the management of the distance between where you are and where the reckoning is waiting. It is the careful, disciplined, expensive work of not arriving at the place where the questions must finally be answered.

Each cycle left residue.

Sharper edges. Narrower patience. Less margin between the person I presented to the world and the pressure building behind the presentation. Control absorbed it. The structure held. The days continued and the kitchens continued and the work continued and from the outside there was nothing to see.

The dreams were patient.

They waited for stillness and took it when it appeared.

The nights continued to assert themselves as a language of their own. Repetition. Escalation. Return. Every time the dreams reappeared, they carried the same message in different forms, pressing closer, refusing to accept containment as a permanent solution, insisting with the quiet inexorable persistence of something that knows it is true and knows you know it too and is simply waiting for you to stop pretending otherwise.

Something unresolved was pressing closer to the surface.

Not asking.

Demanding.

Recognition.

And eventually, in ways that Part I has been building toward since a young Marine lay down in the desert sand and looked up for the first time at three stars in formation, steadily and unmovably present above all the chaos below them, eventually the pressure would find a way through.

Not yet.

But the foundation had been laid.

The break was already in the architecture.

Part I ends here.

But the story does not.

PART II: FEEDING THE CORPS

CHAPTER 7

Cook School

Before going further, it is worth stepping back to trace the path.

Bootcamp. Then Cook School at Parris Island. Then Camp Horno, a grunt unit, infantry, the first real station after school where the education of feeding Marines at volume began. Then WESTPAC, on naval ships, moving through the Philippines and Korea and the ports of the Pacific, the world opening in ways that Parris Island had not prepared for. Then back to Camp Horno. Then the orders that moved everything, reassignment to Las Pulgas with the cannon cockers, the unit that would carry us into the war. Then the desert. Saudi Arabia. Iraq. Kuwait. Desert Storm. Then the return to Las Pulgas on April 8, 1991, the parade deck full of families and an empty space where someone should have been standing.

That is the arc.

Part I lived inside the desert and the return. It examined what the war built and what it left behind and what the body carried home that no order or pamphlet or ceremony acknowledged or addressed.

Part II begins earlier.

At Parris Island.

Where the kitchen first became what everything that followed would depend on.

The pressure had to go somewhere.

That is the part nobody talks about when they describe what happens to a man after war. Not the visible pressure. Not the rage or the grief or the obvious symptoms that get named and documented and treated when they get bad enough to be undeniable. The invisible kind. The kind that lives in the body as a permanent state of readiness, as a nervous system still calibrated for an environment that no longer exists, as an energy with nowhere to go and a man who has promised himself that wherever it goes, it will not be toward the people around him.

The kitchen gave it somewhere to go.

Not immediately. Not with ceremony. The way most important things arrive in a life, it came as an assignment. A set of orders. A destination on a list of destinations, no different in appearance from any other. You reported. You showed up. You found your place in the system and the system told you what was expected.

Cook School wasn't about creativity.

It was about scale.

That distinction mattered more than anyone explained at the time. Most people who cook before they enter a military kitchen are cooking for a table. For a family. For a handful of people whose preferences are known, whose portions are manageable, whose feedback is immediate and personal. Cooking at that scale is intimate. It is about flavor and care and the particular satisfaction of watching someone receive something you made and respond with pleasure.

Cook School at Parris Island had no interest in any of that.

Parris Island is not a place for intimacy. It is a place for transformation. It takes what you bring in and breaks it down to its functional components and rebuilds it according to a different set of requirements. What comes out is not the same as what went in.

That is the point. That is what the institution is designed to produce. And the kitchen, like every other system on that island, operated according to the same logic.

You were not there to cook for one person.

You were not there to cook for ten.

You were there to feed hundreds.

Sometimes thousands.

The adjustment was immediate and physical. The equipment alone was a different language. Industrial ovens that could process volumes your domestic understanding had no frame of reference for. Stock pots the size of what some people used as bathtubs. Sheet pans by the dozens. Knives that saw more use in a single morning than most home kitchens saw in a year. Everything scaled to a dimension that made the cooking you thought you knew feel like a sketch of something, a rough draft of the real thing.

The first lesson was not technique.

It was humility.

You learned very quickly that what you brought with you did not matter as much as what you were willing to learn. The kitchen at that scale had no patience for assumptions. It had no patience for individual style or personal preference or the particular habits you had developed in smaller environments. The kitchen at that scale had one standard and one question: can you produce this correctly, in this quantity, at this time, consistently, day after day, without the quality varying regardless of how tired you are or what else is happening or whether you feel like it today?

Consistency mattered more than personality.

That landed in a specific way for a man who had just returned from the desert carrying the particular kind of internal weather Part I has been describing. Because consistency was something I understood. The watch had been consistency. The sleep that was never fully sleep had been the body's version of consistency. The control that Chapter 5 described in detail was consistency applied to the interior life.

The kitchen rewarded everything the war had already built in me.

It rewarded precision. When you are feeding hundreds of people, a recipe is not a suggestion. It is a specification. The measurements exist for reasons that have nothing to do with preference and everything to do with reliability. The same dish needs to taste the same on Tuesday as it did on Monday as it will on Wednesday. The person eating it on Wednesday should not be able to taste that Tuesday was difficult or that the morning started at two in the morning or that someone on the line was moving slower than they should have been.

Consistency is invisible when it is working.

That is the whole point.

It rewarded attention. In the military kitchen there was always something happening simultaneously at multiple stations, multiple temperatures, multiple stages of preparation feeding into a single coordinated output that had to arrive at the right time, at the right temperature, in the right quantity, without fail. The awareness the watch had installed, the ability to track multiple things without losing the thread of any of them, the capacity to know what was happening at the edge of your attention without making it the center, that was not a liability in this environment.

It was a requirement.

It rewarded the ability to operate without being told.

In a kitchen running at volume you do not wait for instruction between every action. You understand the system well enough to know what comes next. You read the state of the line the way I had learned to read terrain, who was moving efficiently, who was falling behind, where the bottleneck was forming, what adjustment needed to be made before the bottleneck became a problem rather than after.

It rewarded the discipline of doing a thing correctly when no one was watching.

That was the lesson I kept coming back to. The watch from Chapter 2 had no audience. The four hours of darkness and stillness and sustained attention produced nothing visible. No medal. No commendation. No record of whether you drifted or held. The discipline was real only to yourself.

The kitchen had the same quality.

Nobody congratulates you for cleaning a station properly at the end of a shift. Nobody marks it on a record that the mise en place was set up correctly before service began. Nobody acknowledges the hundred small precise things that happen in the background of a well-run kitchen because when they are done correctly they produce only absence. The absence of accidents. The absence of delays. The absence of the failures that announce themselves when the small things have not been attended to.

Presence becomes invisible when it is perfect.

Cook School at Parris Island taught me that the kitchen, like the desert, required everything you had. Not intermittently. Not when you felt like it. Not when the pressure of the day left enough margin for full engagement.

Everything.

All the time.

Your hands had to be where your attention was. The moment attention drifted the moment something began to go wrong in ways that announced themselves at the worst possible time, during service, in front of people counting on the output to sustain them.

Hunger is not abstract when you are feeding Marines.

Marines are working. Marines are training. Marines are operating inside systems that demand physical output and that output requires fuel and the fuel is what comes out of your kitchen three times a day without pause and without reset and without the option of having an off day because you are tired or distracted or still carrying the internal weather that the desert left behind.

The kitchen asked for nothing more and nothing less than everything.

And everything, I was learning, was exactly what I had.

Not because Cook School broke me down and rebuilt me in the way Parris Island was designed to break recruits. I had already been broken down. The desert had done that work more thoroughly than any institutional process could manage. What Cook School gave me was a container for what the desert had built. A system that was demanding enough to require the full deployment of everything that had been installed, precise enough to reward precision, structured enough to give the discipline a legitimate and productive direction.

The pressure had to go somewhere.

The kitchen was where it went.

Not as a decision I made consciously. Not as a calculated choice about career or identity or the particular direction I wanted my life to take. As a recognition that happened in the body before the mind had language for it. The kitchen made sense in the way that very few things made sense in the period after the desert. It asked for what I had. It used what I gave it. It gave back, in the form of a product I could see and measure and improve, the particular kind of satisfaction that comes from a system working correctly because you attended to it correctly.

Hundreds of Marines fed.

Three times a day.

Consistently.

That was the standard.

And consistency, I was discovering, was something I could hold.

Cook School wasn't about creativity.

It was about scale.

And scale, I was learning, was where I was meant to operate.

CHAPTER 8

Camp Horno

Cook School gave you the language.

Camp Horno made you speak it under pressure.

There is a difference between knowing how to do something and knowing how to do it when the margin for error has been removed, when the volume has been multiplied beyond anything the training environment prepared you for, when the people depending on your output are not guests with options but Marines with schedules and missions and a physical requirement for fuel that does not negotiate with how your morning went or whether the delivery came in on time or whether someone on your line is moving at two thirds of the speed they should be.

Camp Pendleton. Camp Horno. A name that meant nothing before it meant everything.

We fed roughly 1,200 Marines.

Three times a day.

Let that number sit for a moment before moving past it because it is easy to read a number and not feel it. 1,200 is not a crowd at a distance. 1,200 is a continuous human demand that begins before most people are awake and does not conclude until after most people have ended their day. 1,200 is a responsibility that does not pause when equipment fails or when the morning crew is short or when the heat in the kitchen has reached a level that makes concentration physically difficult. 1,200 is a standard that exists independently of any circumstances that might argue for lowering it.

Three times a day means the cycle never fully completes before it begins again.

Breakfast concludes and before the last tray has been returned the planning for lunch is already in motion. Lunch concludes and the arc toward dinner has already begun. Dinner concludes and somewhere in the background the preparation for the following morning's breakfast has already started, because breakfast at this scale does not begin at breakfast time. It begins hours before, in the dark, in a kitchen that has not yet been asked to produce anything visible but is already in motion.

No pause.

No reset.

Just flow.

Flow is a word that can sound gentle. Like water moving easily. Like something natural and effortless. What flow means in a kitchen feeding 1,200 Marines three times a day is the opposite of effortless. Flow means the system is so precisely engineered, the roles so clearly understood, the timing so completely internalized, that motion appears continuous even when it is the result of constant conscious effort from every person in the operation. Flow is the absence of visible friction. It is not the absence of work. It is work so well coordinated that the seams don't show.

Getting to flow took time.

The first weeks at Camp Horno were not flow. They were the learning that precedes flow. The particular education that only arrives when the scale is real and the stakes are real and the only way to understand what you do not know is to encounter it directly, in the middle of service, when there is no opportunity to stop and reflect and recalibrate because 1,200 Marines are still eating and the line is still moving and your job is to ensure the output continues regardless of whatever internal recalibration is happening inside you.

You learned what breaks down.

Not in theory. In practice. You learned which parts of the preparation sequence carried the most risk, where the timing was tightest, where a deviation of five minutes in one area created a consequence forty minutes later that felt unrelated until you had seen it enough times to trace the line back. You learned the difference between a problem that could be absorbed without visible impact and a problem that needed to be addressed immediately or it would compound in ways that showed up in the food or in the line or in the faces of the Marines waiting for what your kitchen had committed to producing.

You learned to read the kitchen the way I had learned to read terrain.

The same awareness that Chapter 2 developed on the watch applied here. Not looking for the thing that was already wrong. Looking for the deviation that was becoming wrong. The station that was falling a half step behind. The temperature that was drifting in a direction that would matter in twenty minutes even if it didn't matter yet. The person who was present physically but absent in a way that their output was going to reflect before they recognized it themselves.

You saw it before it announced itself.

That is the difference between someone managing a kitchen and someone running one. Managing is reactive. You respond to what presents itself. Running is anticipatory. You move the pieces before the problem materializes. You make the adjustment before the deviation becomes visible. You maintain the standard not by enforcing it after it has been broken but by creating conditions where breaking it requires more effort than maintaining it.

1,200 Marines three times a day teaches you what maintaining a standard actually requires.

It requires presence. Not the intermittent kind, not the presence you bring when you feel focused and engaged and things are going well. The kind that is constant. That is there at the beginning of the shift when the day is still manageable and the energy is available and at the middle of the shift when the morning's output has already demanded something and the afternoon's output is still ahead and at the end of the shift when the body has been on its feet for hours and the mind has been tracking a dozen things simultaneously for longer than rest has had a chance to restore.

Presence that does not depend on how you feel.

That was the standard Cook School had introduced in language. Camp Horno translated it into the body.

It also taught something about accountability that no classroom could have delivered with the same force.

At that scale, nothing is anonymous.

In a small kitchen, a mistake can be absorbed. It can be caught and corrected and the person who made it can carry the knowledge of it privately, between themselves and whatever standard they hold themselves to. At 1,200 Marines three times a day, nothing disappears quietly. A mistake in preparation shows up in the food. A breakdown in timing shows up in the line. A failure of attention shows up in the output that those 1,200 people put in their bodies and use to sustain the operational requirements of their day.

The food is not abstract.

It is fuel.

And fuel that fails its purpose has consequences that extend beyond the kitchen in ways that the kitchen remains responsible for regardless of how far the chain of consequence travels from the original point of failure.

That understanding changed something.

Not in the dramatic way. Not with ceremony or revelation or a moment I can point to and say that was when the shift happened. The way the most durable changes happen. Gradually. Through repetition. Through doing the thing again and again until the doing of it correctly stopped being something I had to remember to do and became something I did without the memory being required.

The standard internalized.

That is what Camp Horno was really building. Not speed. Not even precision, though both were necessary. The internalization of the standard. The point at which the external requirement and the internal requirement become the same thing. Where you are not maintaining the standard because someone is watching or because the consequence of not maintaining it is too visible to accept. Where you are maintaining it because the alternative has become genuinely unacceptable to you independent of observation or consequence.

That shift matters more than any skill.

Because skill can be present or absent depending on conditions. A person who has skill but has not internalized the standard will deploy the skill when circumstances make it convenient and fall below the standard when circumstances make convenience available.

A person who has internalized the standard does not have that option.

The standard is no longer external. It lives inside. It goes wherever they go. It does not negotiate with convenience or fatigue or the particular difficulty of a given day.

1,200 Marines three times a day.

No pause.

No reset.

Just flow.

And in that flow, in the continuous demanding relentless requirement of that standard applied to that volume day after day, something was being built that would follow me further than Camp Horno. Further than the Marine Corps. Further than the specific kitchens and specific teams and specific operations that would come after.

The discipline of output.

The understanding that the standard exists independently of how you feel about it on a given day.

The particular satisfaction of a system running correctly because everyone inside it is doing their part without being told to and without requiring acknowledgment and without the system needing to pause and address the gap between what was expected and what was delivered.

Flow does not happen by accident.

It is built.

Shift by shift.

Meal by meal.

Marine by Marine.

Until 1,200 becomes a number that no longer represents a challenge.

It represents a responsibility you know how to carry.

CHAPTER 9

San Onofre

Nobody warns you about the moment the number changes.

Camp Horno had been 1,200. Three times a day. The system had been built around that number, calibrated to it, refined through repetition until it ran with the particular smoothness that comes when a team has done something enough times to stop thinking about the individual components and start feeling the whole. 1,200 was a number that had once seemed large and had become, through the specific education of doing it correctly day after day, a number that represented a responsibility understood rather than a challenge endured.

Then the orders came.

San Onofre.

And the number changed.

Now it was 3,000 Marines.

Not 1,200 with adjustments. Not the same operation at a slightly larger scale with the same logic applied more of. Three thousand is not twice twelve hundred. That is the arithmetic and arithmetic is not the point. The point is that scale, when it crosses certain thresholds, does not produce a larger version of what came before. It produces a different category of problem entirely. Problems that did not exist at the lower number, could not have been anticipated from inside the lower number, only visible once you are inside the new scale looking back at what you assumed would transfer and discovering what does not.

Sixteen ovens.

Let that be the image that carries the chapter the way 1,200 carried the last one. Not because sixteen is the number that defines San Onofre but because sixteen ovens running simultaneously is a specific and concrete representation of what 3,000 Marines three times a day actually requires in physical space and physical heat and physical coordination among people who must each be doing their part precisely at the right moment for the aggregate output to arrive on time at the right temperature in the right quantity without visible evidence of the complexity that produced it.

Sixteen ovens.

Each one a variable. Each one a timeline with a beginning and a specific window and a consequence for missing the window that compounds into the timelines of everything adjacent. The oven to the left running two minutes behind is not a two minute problem. It is a cascade. It affects the station drawing from it, which affects the line that station feeds into, which affects the timing of an output that 3,000 people are waiting for on a schedule that does not adjust for internal kitchen complications.

Sixteen variables. Simultaneously. Continuously. Without pause.

This is where I learned control at volume.

Not control in the sense Chapter 5 described. Not the interior containment of a man managing the psychological weather of the war he carried home. That kind of control had found the kitchen as its most legitimate outlet, had settled into the structure and precision and forward momentum of culinary work as the place where the discipline installed by the desert could produce something rather than simply hold something in place.

This was different.

This was control as a professional practice. As a system. As the specific learned capacity to hold sixteen variables in attention simultaneously, to know where each one was in its timeline, to anticipate where each one was going, to make the adjustment before the adjustment became necessary and visible rather than after it had already cost something.

The desert had taught this in one form.

San Onofre translated it into another.

In the desert, awareness had to span a perimeter. You held the position you were responsible for while tracking the positions adjacent to yours while remaining available to the wider operational picture without losing the particular focus your position required. You could not be fully absorbed in one direction because threat did not always announce its direction in advance. You had to be distributed without being diffuse. Present everywhere your responsibility reached without being absent at its center.

Sixteen ovens required the same quality of distributed presence.

You could not stand at one oven and manage it perfectly while the other fifteen operated on faith. You could not assign your full attention to the station that was behind and trust that the station that was on time would stay on time without attention. Attention at volume is not a spotlight. It is ambient. It covers the space. It registers deviation before deviation has fully formed.

The body learned this before the mind could articulate it.

That is how deep learning always arrives. Not as a concept you understand and then apply. As a capacity you develop through repetition until it operates below conscious effort, until the tracking happens automatically the way breathing happens automatically, until you are not deciding to monitor the kitchen but simply monitoring it the way a body simply maintains its temperature, without instruction, without acknowledgment, as a continuous background function that sustains everything else.

The team mattered here in a way it had not at the same level before.

At 1,200 the team was essential. At 3,000 the team was everything. One person could not hold sixteen timelines simultaneously no matter how refined the awareness or how internalized the standard. The distributed presence required to run a kitchen at that volume had to be distributed literally, across multiple people, each one holding their portion of the system with the same standard the whole system required, so that what the leader was actually managing was not the kitchen directly but the people running it.

That distinction is where leadership begins to separate from management.

Management is direct. You manage the task. You manage the timeline. You manage the output. Your attention is on the work itself and the work responds to your attention.

Leadership is mediated. You lead the people who are managing the tasks and the timelines and the outputs. Your attention is on them. Your understanding of the work is what allows you to assess whether their management of it is sufficient. Your standard is the reference point against which their performance is measured. But you are not doing the work. You are ensuring the work is done correctly by people who have internalized the standard well enough to do it correctly without you at their shoulder.

San Onofre was where this distinction became real.

Not as a theory I had been taught. As a necessity I could not operate without. You could not run a kitchen feeding 3,000 Marines three times a day by being present at every station simultaneously. You had to build people who could run their stations without you. Who understood the standard well enough to hold it when you were not watching. Who could make the adjustment in real time without waiting for instruction because waiting for instruction at that volume introduces a delay the system cannot absorb.

This required trust.

Trust built on evidence. Not assumption, not hope, not the goodwill of good intentions. Evidence. You watched how people worked when the pressure was low and used that as your prediction for how they would work when the pressure was high. You paid attention to who asked questions versus who asked the same question twice. Who caught their own mistakes versus who needed the mistakes pointed out. Who raised the problem while it was still manageable versus who stayed quiet until it had grown.

You learned to see people the way the watch had taught you to see terrain.

Not what was visible. What was indicated. The deviation before it became a problem. The pattern before it produced a consequence.

Sixteen ovens.

Three thousand Marines.

Three times a day.

No pause. No reset.

And in that environment, feeding Marines was not simply a culinary function. It was a logistics operation. A precision exercise. A continuous test of whether the standard had been internalized deeply enough to hold under the specific pressure of its highest demand.

Hot food arrived to the line on time.

Not because it was easy.

Because the people responsible for it had been built to a standard that made on time the only acceptable outcome regardless of the difficulty of the path to get there.

That was the lesson San Onofre delivered that no smaller environment could have produced.

Control at volume is not the same as control.

Control at volume requires that the standard live in everyone, not just the person responsible for the standard. It requires that the culture of the kitchen carry the expectation so completely that individual compliance is not compliance at all but simply how people who belong to that kitchen operate as a matter of identity.

Not because they are told to.

Because they have internalized it.

Because the kitchen has become who they are, not just where they work.

I was learning to build that.

Not yet with full understanding of what I was building. Not with the language I have now for what was happening. But in the body. In the practice. In the particular daily education of running sixteen ovens feeding 3,000 Marines and discovering, shift by shift, what control at volume actually requires.

It requires more than skill.

It requires people.

And building people, I was beginning to understand, was the real work.

But before I fully understood that, there was a morning that taught me something else first.

Something about what I was actually capable of when the full demand of the environment was placed on one person operating alone.

Breakfast at San Onofre.

The bacon.

I don't remember exactly how it came to be that I was running it solo that morning. What I remember is the decision. The sixteen ovens. The sheet pans. The particular arithmetic of what feeding 3,000 Marines for breakfast actually required in terms of bacon, which is not a small number when the number of people eating it is that large.

Each oven held six full size sheet pans.

Each sheet pan held approximately thirty strips of bacon laid out in rows, the fat distributed across the pan in a way that would render correctly under heat, that would produce the color and the texture and the crispness that the standard required without going past it into the territory where bacon becomes something other than what it is supposed to be.

Thirty strips per pan.

Six pans per oven.

One hundred and eighty strips per oven.

Sixteen ovens.

Two thousand eight hundred and eighty strips of bacon.

All at once.

I loaded them myself. Pan by pan, oven by oven, working through the sequence with the particular focus that the scale required. Not the focus of someone trying to manage a situation that exceeds their capacity. The focus of someone who has internalized the standard deeply enough that the scale is not a source of anxiety but a source of clarity. Clarity about exactly what needs to happen, in exactly what sequence, at exactly what timing, for the output to arrive correctly.

Because if any of it burned I stayed.

Day on. Stay on.

That was not a threat I was trying to avoid. It was a standard I was trying to uphold. The distinction matters because the motivation behind the focus changes what the focus produces. Avoiding consequence produces a different quality of attention than honoring a standard. Avoiding consequence makes you careful. Honoring a standard makes you precise.

I was precise.

I tracked sixteen timelines simultaneously. Each oven in a different phase of its cycle, each phase requiring a different response or no response at all, the whole operation a continuous distributed awareness of where every piece of that output was in its arc from raw to finished without a single piece crossing the line from finished into burned.

Two thousand eight hundred and eighty strips of bacon.

Not one burned.

I did not celebrate it. There was no moment of standing back and marking what had just been accomplished. The line needed to be fed. The next task was already present. You move forward.

But that morning stayed with me.

Not as pride in the conventional sense. As information. As the particular knowledge, arrived at through practice rather than instruction, that what I was capable of when the full demand of an environment was placed on me was something beyond what most people in that kitchen could do. That the combination of focus and distributed awareness and precision under pressure and absolute commitment to the standard was not common.

It was foundational.

I did not have language for it then. I did not have a name for what had been built in me across Cook School and Camp Horno and those sixteen ovens and the 2 a.m. starts and the particular education of being required to perform at a level the institution had not yet officially recognized.

Years later, in civilian kitchens, in professional environments, in the culinary career that would follow the Marine Corps and build on everything the Marine Corps had forged, people would encounter what that morning had produced. They would encounter the focus and the precision and the ability to hold a complex operation in full awareness without losing any part of it and they would have their own names for it.

But it was built here.

In a military kitchen at San Onofre.

At 2 a.m.

Across sixteen ovens.

With 2,880 pieces of bacon and not one of them burned.

That is the making of a Maestro.

Everything else was preparation for that.

CHAPTER 10

Day On, Stay On

The kitchen at 2 a.m. is a different place than the kitchen at noon.

Not in the physical sense. The equipment is the same. The stations are the same. The ovens and the pots and the sheet pans and the particular institutional smell of a military kitchen that has absorbed years of production into its walls and its surfaces and its ventilation, all of that is identical at 2 a.m. to what it is at any other hour.

What is different is everything that surrounds the kitchen.

At noon the base is awake. There is movement and noise and the ambient presence of a functioning institution going about its daytime business. Light comes through the windows. People pass outside. The world is operating on a schedule that acknowledges the hour and responds to it with the energy appropriate to the middle of a day.

At 2 a.m. none of that is true.

At 2 a.m. the world outside the kitchen has gone somewhere else. The base has quieted to its overnight version of itself, which is not silent but is a particular kind of reduced, a dimming of the operational intensity that characterizes the daylight hours, a concession to the biological requirement of the people who live inside it that some hours will be less demanded than others.

The kitchen does not make that concession.

Breakfast started at 2 a.m.

That sentence is simple and its simplicity is almost misleading because what it contains is not simple at all. Breakfast started at 2 a.m. means that the people responsible for breakfast were in the kitchen before 2 a.m. They were in the kitchen at 1 a.m. or earlier, depending on the volume and the complexity of what breakfast required that particular morning. They were in the kitchen when the base was at its quietest, when the pull toward remaining horizontal was at its most persuasive, when the body's argument that rest was still available and that the standard could wait another hour was at its most compelling because no one outside the kitchen would see them waiting or know the difference in the hour they chose to begin.

No one outside the kitchen.

But 3,000 Marines would experience the difference at 0600.

That understanding is what the standard requires. Not the visible accountability of someone watching to see whether you arrived on time. The invisible accountability of the consequence that lives downstream of your choice, in the quality of what arrives at the line at the hour the line requires it, in the temperature of what 3,000 people put in their bodies to fuel the day the institution has planned for them. The accountability that exists whether or not anyone traces the morning's food back to the hour the kitchen began.

2 a.m. is the price of that accountability.

You paid it or you didn't.

And if you didn't, the kitchen had its own accounting system.

If you burned something, you stayed.

That is not a long sentence. It contains a complete philosophy in five words and a period. It requires no elaboration to be understood intellectually. But intellectual understanding and the understanding that lives in the body after you have experienced its application are two different kinds of knowing and the kitchen at Camp Horno and San Onofre was interested only in the second kind.

If you burned something, you meant you had failed a basic requirement of the standard. You had allowed something in your care to exceed its limit. You had been inattentive or impatient or simply present in the kitchen without being present in the particular way the kitchen required, your hands where your attention was, your awareness distributed across your responsibilities, your monitoring continuous rather than intermittent.

Burning something was not an accident.

Burning something was information.

It told the kitchen something about the person who had burned it. It told the kitchen that this person's presence in the operation at the level the operation required was not yet reliable enough to be trusted without consequence. It told the kitchen that the cost of the inattention had not yet been high enough to produce the change the standard demanded.

And so the kitchen raised the cost.

You stayed.

Not as punishment in the theatrical sense. Not as humiliation designed to wound or diminish. As education delivered in the only language that produces durable learning: consequence. The consequence had to be proportional to the lesson. The lesson was that the standard existed independently of how the person responsible for meeting it felt about meeting it at any given moment.

The lesson was that excellence was not an aspiration you maintained when conditions were favorable and set aside when they were not.

The lesson was that the standard did not care about your circumstances.

Staying meant you completed your shift and then you stayed to do more. When your crew was preparing to leave, to change out of the uniform that smelled like the morning's work, to eat their own meal, to move toward the part of the day that belonged to them rather than to the kitchen, you stayed. You stayed because the kitchen had not received from you what the kitchen was owed. Because excellence is not partially delivered and then settled at a discount. Because the hour you owed the standard was still outstanding and the only way to close that account was to pay it.

Day on.

Stay on.

Four words. The complete expression of an accountability philosophy that required no further explanation because it explained itself through its application. You saw it happen to others before you experienced it yourself. You watched someone burn something and understood immediately what was coming and watched the understanding land in the room before the words were spoken. You watched the staying. You watched the kitchen continue to operate while one person's day extended past the boundary everyone else crossed.

You did not want to be that person.

Not because of the staying itself, though the staying was real and it was demanding and it arrived at a point in the shift when the body had already produced a full day's worth of output and the invitation to stop was not theoretical but physical and immediate.

Because of what the staying meant.

The staying meant your attention had been insufficient. Your care had been incomplete. Your presence in the kitchen, the particular quality of presence that the kitchen required at all times from everyone operating inside it, had not been what the kitchen was owed from a person who understood what the kitchen was and what it was for and who was depending on it.

3,000 Marines.

Three times a day.

That number sat in the background of every shift. It did not need to be invoked. It did not require a speech or a reminder or a motivational accounting of what was at stake. It was simply true. The Marines eating breakfast at 0600 were fueling a day of training and operation and the physical demands of military service. The quality of the fuel mattered. The temperature mattered. Whether it arrived on time mattered. Whether it had been produced with the precision and care that the standard required mattered.

None of that was abstract.

None of that was negotiable.

And so the accountability system that governed the kitchen was not separate from the mission. It was the mission in its most operational form. The consequence of burning something and staying to make it right was not the institution protecting its standards for institutional reasons. It was the kitchen insisting on the quality that 3,000 people depended on and refusing to accept a version of service that was less than what those people had coming.

This is where the discipline of Chapter 2 and the internalized standard of Chapters 7, 8, and 9 arrived at their practical test.

The watch had required attention when nothing was happening.

The kitchen at 2 a.m. required attention when the body's argument for something other than attention was at its loudest. When fatigue was real and sleep was recent memory and the shift ahead was visible in its full length and the only reason to bring full presence to it was the standard itself and the people downstream of the standard who would experience what the standard produced.

You brought full presence because they deserved it.

Not because you were being observed.

Not because the consequence of falling short was visible in advance.

Because the work deserved it and the people the work served deserved it and the standard that made the work mean something deserved it.

That understanding does not arrive as a concept.

It arrives through 2 a.m.

Through the particular discipline of beginning when the world has not yet begun. Through the accountability of knowing that what you produce in the hours no one sees will be experienced in full by the people who depend on you at the hours they are present.

Through the education of Day On, Stay On.

Not as a rule imposed from outside.

As a standard you eventually carry inside.

Because that is the only version of the standard that actually holds.

The version that does not require enforcement.

The version that is simply who you are in a kitchen.

At any hour.

Under any pressure.

With or without anyone watching.

That was what the 2 a.m. kitchen built.

Not through gentleness.

Through the specific grace of consequence applied consistently, without exception, to anyone who had not yet learned what the kitchen required.

Day on.

Stay on.

Until the standard is no longer something you remember to hold.

It is simply something you are.

CHAPTER 11

Master Sergeant Overton

Before Overton arrived, we were doing the job.

That is the most honest description of what the mess hall was before he walked into it. We were doing the job. We were showing up and feeding Marines and running the shifts and meeting the operational requirements and doing all of the things that the position required with a competence that was sufficient and a culture that was comfortable and a standard that was, if you measured it against the basic requirement of the mission, acceptable.

Acceptable.

That word sat in the mess hall like furniture nobody questioned. Not uncomfortable enough to remove. Not impressive enough to mention. Just there. Part of the environment. The particular ambient standard of a kitchen that had never been asked to be anything other than what it was and had responded by being exactly what it was and nothing more.

We were cooks.

We worked.

We fed Marines.

We partied.

We moved through the system.

We had camaraderie among ourselves, the particular closeness that develops among people who share difficult early mornings and long shifts and the physical intimacy of shared work in a hot and demanding environment. That was real. That had value. The culture of the mess hall was not broken. It was not hostile or careless or deliberately below standard.

It simply had no direction above itself.

We were not striving to be the best.

We were doing the job.

That ended when he arrived.

The change didn't happen gradually.

It walked in.

Master Sergeant Overton took over the mess hall after the previous top retired. We were lined up when we first met him. New leadership always brings a certain quality of attention, a suspended assessment that operates in the first moments before the new person has said or done enough to tell you what category of leader they belong to. Some arrivals answer that question quickly. Some take longer.

Overton answered it immediately.

Not through volume. Not through the particular display of authority that some leaders use to establish position before they have established credibility. He didn't need to establish position because his presence did that without assistance. He stood in front of us and the room reorganized itself around where he was standing without anyone deciding to let it.

He had come from the East Coast. South Carolina, from what I remember. That carried a different presence. A different cadence. A different expectation. Most of us were from places like St. Louis, Virginia, Philadelphia. Urban. Fast. Direct. We moved and spoke with the particular efficiency of people who had learned to communicate a lot in a short amount of space because space, in the environments we came from, was something you competed for.

He brought something else.

Grounded. Controlled. Certain.

And more than anything else, intentional.

There is a difference between a person who is deliberate and a person who is intentional. Deliberate means measured. It means careful. It means the actions are considered before they are taken. Intentional means something deeper. It means the actions are connected to a purpose that operates behind them, that gives them direction and coherence, that makes them part of something larger than the individual action itself. Intentional means you are not just doing what the situation requires. You are building toward something.

Overton was building toward something from the first day.

He didn't waste time.

Right from the beginning he laid out the roadmap.

"We're going to be the best mess hall on Camp Pendleton."

Four words after the verb. The best. Not among the better ones. Not above average. Not improved from where we currently stood. The best.

Not a suggestion.

Not motivation offered in the hope that some of it would stick.

A standard.

At the time Camp Pendleton had multiple mess halls. Each one feeding its own units, operating under the same basic mission, producing the same basic output, measuring itself against the same basic requirement that the mission was met and the Marines were fed and the operation continued. In that landscape, every mess hall was essentially equal because every mess hall was meeting the minimum.

Overton did not see us as one mess hall among many meeting the minimum.

He saw us as the one.

And for us, that mattered in a way that is difficult to explain to someone who has not experienced what happens to a group of people when someone looks at them and sees something they have not yet seen in themselves. We were not just being led. We were being seen. We were being told that what we were capable of was more than what we had been producing. That the gap between where we were and where we could be was not a distance we could not cross but a distance we had simply not yet been asked to cross.

He was also the first copper colored Master Sergeant we had leading the mess hall. American Indian in presence and bearing, with something in the way he carried himself that felt older than rank, older than the institution, rooted in something the institution had not given him and could not take away.

That was not a small detail.

It was an honor. It carried pride that arrived before anything else changed, before a single standard had been raised or a single improvement had been made. There was something in his presence that said the room was capable of more than it had been given credit for. Not because of what he said. Because of what his being there meant.

That pride mattered.

It changed what people were willing to do before they understood why they were willing to do it.

Then the work began.

He didn't raise his voice.

He raised the standard.

Those two sentences need to be understood together because the relationship between them is the heart of what Overton introduced. A leader who raises their voice is responding to a gap between where things are and where they should be. The voice is the signal that the gap has become unacceptable. But the gap persists. The voice addresses the symptom. It does not address the cause. When the voice stops the gap is still there, waiting for the next provocation.

Overton understood that the gap was not a behavior problem.

It was a standard problem.

The mess hall was not performing below standard because the people in it were incapable or unwilling. It was performing at the level of the standard it had been given and had given itself. The standard was the problem. Raise the standard and the performance follows. Not immediately. Not without resistance. But fundamentally, because people rise to the level of what is expected of them when the expectation is genuine and consistent and held without exception.

No more good enough.

No more getting through the shift.

If you fried chicken it had to be the best fried chicken on Camp Pendleton. Not acceptable fried chicken. Not fried chicken that met the requirement. The best. If you baked chicken it had to be the best. If you made a salad that salad bar had to be the best any Marine would see anywhere on that installation.

Everything mattered.

Not just the outcome.

The approach.

Uniforms had to be right. Not approximately right. Not right on the days when inspection was possible. Right. Stations had to be clean. Presentation had to be tight. Execution had to be consistent from the first service of the day to the last. There was no separation between small things and big things because everything reflected the standard and the standard did not have tiers. It did not reserve its full expression for the visible moments and relax its grip on the invisible ones.

The standard was the standard.

Everywhere. Always.

When the standard rises, people either fall away or they rise with it.

We rose.

It took time. It required the particular discomfort of being asked to operate at a level above what had previously been sufficient and discovering the distance between that level and where you currently stood. It required the adjustment period where the new expectation and the existing capacity have not yet aligned and the gap between them produces friction and frustration and the specific kind of exhaustion that comes not from overwork but from running a standard that your system has not yet fully incorporated.

But the culture shifted.

You could feel it before you could measure it.

The way the kitchen felt at the beginning of a shift changed. The attention brought to preparation changed. The particular care applied to the small things, the things no one was specifically watching, the things that would never appear in any evaluation or report, changed. Not because anyone was enforcing the standard at that level of detail but because the standard had begun to internalize. Because the culture of the mess hall had started to reorganize itself around a different center of gravity.

Excellence instead of adequacy.

It didn't take long before the difference showed.

Word spread.

When dignitaries came to Camp Pendleton they didn't rotate through mess halls anymore. They came to ours. Generals. Command staff. Special events tied to parades and major operations. When those moments happened, they happened at Pulgas. And when they came, they ate our food.

That wasn't assigned.

That was earned.

And Overton made sure it was recognized. He didn't allow what we did to be minimized. We weren't just cooks. We were professionals feeding Marines. There is a difference. The difference is not in the task itself but in the relationship the person performing the task has with the standard they bring to it. A cook produces food. A professional feeding Marines understands that the food is fuel for people who need it to function at the level their mission requires, and brings to its production the same seriousness that any professional brings to work that matters for reasons beyond the personal.

He made sure everyone understood that difference.

What he did wasn't just operational.

It was cultural.

He took a group of young Marines who were doing the job, who were moving through the system with the particular combination of competence and comfort that acceptable produces, and gave them something higher to operate inside of.

Pride.

Not loud pride. Not the pride that announces itself and seeks acknowledgment. Not ego wearing the mask of professional identity.

Earned pride.

The kind that shows up in how you carry yourself when no one is watching. How you show up to your station at 2 a.m. when the only person who will know whether you were fully present is you. How you prepare food that most people will consume without a second thought, without recognition of the care that went into it, without any awareness of the standard it represented.

The pride of doing excellent work because excellent work is what the work deserves.

That was new.

For me it landed differently than it did for others in the room.

Because by the time Overton arrived, I had already proven I could handle volume. San Onofre had shown that. Camp Horno had shaped it. I had the capacity. I understood the scale. I could run the operation.

But capacity without direction is just potential.

Overton gave it direction.

He introduced something I hadn't fully locked into yet.

Striving for excellence.

Not being the best compared to others, which is a moving target that depends on who else is in the room and what they are bringing on a given day. But holding yourself to a standard that doesn't change regardless of who else is in the room or what they are bringing.

That distinction matters.

Being the best depends on comparison.

Excellence depends on standard.

And standard is internal.

Standard is the thing you carry. The thing that goes where you go. The thing that determines the quality of your work in environments where no one else's work is visible for comparison. Standard is what you bring when you are the only one there to hold it.

That shift in understanding changed something that could not be changed back.

Looking back that was the first time in my culinary life where something moved from, I can do this to I am going to do this at the highest level possible. Not for recognition. Not for rank. Not because the external reward for excellence exceeded the external reward for adequacy, which it often does not. For the standard itself. Because the work deserved the standard and the people the work served deserved the standard and the person, I was becoming deserved to carry a standard that reflected what I was actually capable of.

Overton didn't build my ability.

That was already there.

He refined it.

He gave it structure.

He gave it expectation.

He gave it purpose.

And under that purpose, inside that structure, held by that expectation, the mess hall became what he said it would become on the first day he stood in front of us.

The best mess hall on Camp Pendleton.

Not by chance.

By design.

His design, at the beginning.

And then ours.

Because that is what genuine leadership produces.

Not dependence on the leader.

Independence that carries the leader's standard forward after the leader is no longer in the room.

Not because you were told to.

Because you understood why it mattered.

And understanding why something matters is the difference between following a standard and owning one.

Overton gave me ownership.

Everything that came after was built on that.

CHAPTER 12

Chief Cook

The opportunity arrived the way most real opportunities arrive.

Not announced. Not framed as an opportunity at the time it appeared. As a gap. A space in the operation that needed to be filled and that no one at the appropriate rank was positioned to fill and that the mission could not allow to remain empty regardless of the rank attached to whoever filled it.

Two Staff Sergeants rotated out.

That was it. No ceremony around the departure. No formal designation of what their leaving created. They were there and then they were not there and the kitchen that had been running with their presence in those roles now needed to run without it.

I was an E-3.

The billet was for an E-6.

Three grades of separation between what the position required on paper and what was standing in front of it in practice. Three grades that represented, in the language of the institution, three levels of rank, three levels of accumulated authority, three levels of official certification that the person holding them had been assessed and advanced and recognized as ready for the responsibilities those grades carried.

I did not have any of that.

What I had was the standard Overton had given me, the capacity that San Onofre had built, the understanding of what the kitchen required that Camp Horno had produced and that the 2 a.m. shifts had installed in the body rather than simply the mind. What I had was the particular combination of ability and internalized standard that Chapters 7 through 11 had been building toward, present in a person who had not yet been given the rank to match it.

You don't wait for permission to lead.

You step into it.

Not as a declaration. Not as a performance of confidence for the room. As a recognition of what the situation required and a decision, made quietly and without fanfare, to be what the situation required regardless of what the official record said about whether I was supposed to be that yet.

Overton had made it clear.

If you stepped forward the opportunity would be there.

This was the opportunity.

Sixteen Marines under me.

Sixteen people whose output would now reflect my leadership. Whose work in the kitchen would be shaped by the standard I held and the expectation I communicated and the culture I either built or failed to build. Sixteen people who would rise to what I required of them or settle into what I was willing to accept. Sixteen people who would tell me, through the quality of their daily work, whether I had understood Overton's lesson or simply heard it.

The first lesson arrived before I had time to find my footing.

My crew left the kitchen half done on cleanup.

Not dramatically. Not defiantly. With the casual acceptance of a standard that had not yet been required to be higher. They had done enough to technically be done and had moved toward the door and the meal that was waiting for them and the rest that came after a shift and the entirely human desire to be finished with work when work is nominally finished.

The kitchen told a different story.

Surfaces that should have been clean were not fully clean. Stations that should have been reset for the next shift were not fully reset. The kind of cleanup that represents the kitchen as the incoming team will find it rather than as the outgoing team is comfortable leaving it had not happened.

My two Sergeants called me into the office.

My crew was out eating breakfast. I was in that office, across from men who outranked me, who had watched the operation longer than I had been running it, who had seen young leaders come through this kitchen and had a particular understanding of what the first real test looks like and what it reveals.

They did not ease into it.

They chastised me.

Directly. Without softening. In the language that the Marine Corps uses when it wants to ensure that the message lands in the body and not just the mind. They told me what had happened. They told me what it meant. They told me that my crew's performance reflected my leadership and that my leadership had, in this instance, fallen short of what the kitchen required.

And then they told me to get down.

Pushups.

Not as humiliation. As calibration. As the particular physical language, the Corps uses to bring a person back to the body, to the physical reality of what is being asked of them, to the understanding that leadership is not an intellectual exercise but a physical commitment. You feel it. You carry it in the muscles. You stand up from it with a knowledge in the body that the mind alone cannot produce.

I pushed until I could not push anymore.

And while I was pushing, they were talking.

Not stopping to let me focus on the floor. Talking. Mentoring. Telling me what I needed to know while my arms were failing so that the lesson arrived at the exact moment of maximum physical vulnerability. So that it could not be filed away for later consideration. So that it entered at the moment the body had no defenses left and settled in the way that things settle when there is nothing left to resist them.

They told me that my crew had disrespected my authority.

Not loudly. Not dramatically. Through the quiet assumption that the standard I held was not high enough to make falling below it uncomfortable. Through the particular casual carelessness of people who have not yet been given a reason to take the person they are accountable to seriously.

They told me that the disrespect was mine to address.

Not theirs.

Mine.

Because that is what leadership means at the level I had stepped into. The failures of the people below you do not belong to them alone. They belong to the leader. The leader's job is to create conditions where the failure is not acceptable to the people who might otherwise commit it. Where the cost of falling short is higher than the cost of meeting the standard. Where the culture of the kitchen makes cutting corners not a temptation to manage but an impossibility to consider.

I had not yet built that culture.

This was the lesson for how to build it.

I walked out of that office and went directly to work.

I took the Cadillac to the wet room.

The Cadillac is the large wheeled mop bucket, the piece of equipment you move through a kitchen when you are doing the kind of cleaning that is not routine maintenance but thorough reckoning. I filled six stainless steel trash cans with soapy water. Not one. Not two. Six. Enough to do what I had decided needed to be done in a way that could not be misunderstood as anything other than what it was.

And then I drowned the kitchen.

From the tables down.

The entire kitchen, flooded with soapy water from the surfaces to the floor, cleaned in a way that went past the standard and into the territory that leaves no question about what the standard actually is. Not the minimum required. The maximum possible. The kind of clean that takes time and effort and communicates through the physical reality of its result exactly where the bar has been set.

The cooks walked back in with their dirty plates.

Ready to turn them in and get off work.

Ready to move toward the rest of the day.

They walked into a kitchen that looked nothing like the one they had left.

They walked into water. Into the unmistakable evidence that while they had been eating breakfast someone had been in their kitchen doing the work they had decided not to do. Into the clear and wordless communication that the person now responsible for this kitchen had a different definition of finished than the one they had been operating under.

I didn't give a speech.

I didn't need to.

The kitchen gave it for me.

I told them what had happened and what was going to happen next.

They were going to reclean the kitchen. All of it. To the standard the kitchen was now going to be held to, which was the standard they should have held it to the first time.

The last thing you want when you are ready to get off work and go eat and go party and have the part of the day that belongs to you is two extra hours of work that could have been avoided by doing the job correctly the first time.

That was the point.

Not two hours of punishment. Two hours of consequence. Two hours that belonged to the standard and that had been borrowed without permission and that now needed to be returned with interest because that is how accountability works when it is applied honestly.

It never happened again.

That last sentence is the one that matters most. Not the water. Not the pushups. Not the office or the Sergeants or the particular education of being chastised while the crew you are responsible for is eating your mistakes. All of that was instruction. The instruction was real and it was necessary and it is the reason this story belongs in this chapter.

But the sentence that matters is the one that comes after.

It never happened again.

Because that is what genuine accountability produces. Not resentment. Not compliance maintained under threat that dissolves the moment the threat is absent. Recalibration. A shared understanding of where the standard actually is and what it actually requires and what the cost of falling below it will be regardless of whether anyone happens to be watching when the decision to fall below it presents itself.

The kitchen changed after that day.

Not because of fear. Because of clarity.

Because my crew understood, from that point forward, what I understood. That the kitchen was not a place where the minimum was the standard. That the work we did in it had a downstream human consequence that did not negotiate with how tired you were or how ready you were to be done. That the person leading them had been built by Overton and San Onofre and the 2 a.m. shifts and the particular education of having carried more weight than the rank on his collar said he should be carrying and had brought that standard into this kitchen and was not going to lower it for the convenience of people who had not yet been required to rise to it.

No rank to protect me.

Respect had to be earned.

Every shift.

Through the consistency of the standard held and the accountability applied and the culture-built day by day out of the choices made at every small decision point where it was easier to let something go than to address it.

That is where leadership started.

Not from title.

Not from rank.

From responsibility.

From the specific willingness to step into a role three grades above where the institution said you belonged, to take full ownership of what happened inside that role, to address what needed to be addressed in the way it needed to be addressed without waiting for permission or approval or the official certification that you were ready.

An E-3 running an E-6 billet.

Sixteen Marines under me.

Managing output. Orders. Execution.

The standard Overton had given me now given to them.

Not by telling them about it.

By requiring it.

By being the example of it before I required it of anyone else.

By filling six trash cans with soapy water and drowning the kitchen so that when they walked back in there was no question about what kind of leader had taken this role or what standard they were now being held to or what the cost of falling below it was going to be.

You don't wait for permission to lead.

You step into it.

And then you hold the standard you stepped into as if you always belonged there.

Because eventually you do.

Not because the institution decides you do.

Because the people around you can feel it in how you carry yourself and how you run your kitchen and how you respond when the standard is not met and how you make clear, without cruelty but without apology, that the standard is not optional.

That is what the E-6 billet required.

That is what I brought to it.

Not because I had been told I was ready.

Because the kitchen needed what I had.

And I had stopped waiting to be told that was enough.

PART III: WESTPAC

CHAPTER 13

WestPac The Ship

After Camp Horno and San Onofre and the E-6 billet and the particular education of Part II, WESTPAC arrived the way everything in the Marine Corps arrived.

As orders.

No announcement that something important was beginning. No ceremony to mark the transition from the land-based life of the kitchen to something larger and less defined. Gear packed. Movement. Time zones beginning to lose their meaning as the aircraft carried us away from the familiar rhythms of Camp Pendleton and into the particular suspension that travel produces in a person who does not know yet what they are traveling toward.

We were split across ships.

I ended up on the smallest one in the fleet.

An LST.

Landing Ship Tank. Flat-bottomed. Designed not for comfort or for speed but for utility, for the specific operational function of delivering tanks and vehicles and Marines onto beaches that deeper-hulled ships could not approach. The design that made it useful for its mission made it responsive to the ocean in a way that larger ships were not. A deep-hulled vessel cuts through water. An LST rides on top of it. The distinction between those two relationships with the ocean is not abstract when you are standing in a galley trying to cook.

When the ocean moved, we moved with it.

Not metaphorically. Physically. The deck shifted under your feet with the particular unpredictability of a surface that is negotiating constantly with something far larger and far older than itself. The Pacific Ocean has no interest in the schedule of a military kitchen. It has no interest in whether the pans are level or whether the liquids stay in the pots or whether the person trying to prepare food for the Marines aboard can find a stable position from which to work.

It simply moves.

And everything on the ship moves with it.

The first days in that galley were an education in the difference between skill and adaptability. Cook School at Parris Island had built skill. Camp Horno and San Onofre had refined it. Skill is the mastery of technique in a controlled environment; the internalized standard applied to conditions that are demanding but stable. The deck does not move at Camp Horno. The ovens do not shift. The relationship between your body and the surface you are working on does not change from one moment to the next.

On the LST it changed constantly.

Pans slid if you left them unattended for a moment too long. Liquids moved in their containers in ways that turned standard techniques into problems requiring solutions that no recipe had anticipated. The relationship between heat and food that you had learned on land operated differently when the vessel carrying the heat source was itself in motion. You could not assume that what had worked five minutes ago would work now. The conditions were always shifting. The only constant was the shifting itself.

You had two options.

Fight it or move with it.

Fighting it meant spending your energy in opposition to a force you could not overcome. The ocean was not going to stop moving because a cook in a military galley needed a stable surface. Fighting it produced exhaustion and broken equipment and food that reflected the struggle rather than the standard. Fighting it meant you were at war with your environment instead of operating inside it.

Moving with it meant something different.

It meant reading the movement before you responded to it. Feeling the deck shift and adjusting your stance before the shift cost you anything. Keeping your weight distributed in a way that could absorb the next motion without losing balance. Working with the rhythm of the ship rather than against it, timing your movements to the intervals between the larger rolls, using the moments of relative stability to accomplish what needed to be accomplished and holding position through the instability rather than fighting to restore a stability that was never going to return.

You didn't fight it. You moved with it.

That's how you stayed upright.

And kept everything under control.

The lesson was not only about cooking.

It was about the nature of control itself. Part I had described control as a container, a sealed system that held internal pressure in place by building walls strong enough to resist it. Part II had described control as a professional standard, the internalized expectation that produced consistent output regardless of conditions.

The ship introduced a third dimension.

Control that was not resistance but adaptation. Control that did not try to hold the environment still but moved with it intelligently. Control that understood the difference between what could be managed and what had to be accommodated, between the conditions you could shape and the conditions you had to work inside of.

The ocean could not be shaped.

It could only be read and responded to.

That understanding settled into the body the way all understanding settles when the body is the one doing the learning. Not as a concept I could articulate. As a physical adjustment that became second nature over days and then weeks at sea. The stance widened slightly, weight lower, the center of gravity adjusted downward to widen the base. The hands learned to hold differently, a lighter grip that could give with unexpected movement rather than a tight grip that would resist it and transfer the force upward through the arms.

The kitchen on that ship was not large.

It was exactly the size it needed to be and no larger. Everything in it had a place that existed for operational rather than aesthetic reasons. The equipment was secured. The storage was designed around the assumption of motion. The people working in it had to learn to move around each other in a space that was already demanding adaptation from each individual before it asked them to coordinate with everyone else in it simultaneously.

The team on that ship became something different than a kitchen team on land.

On land, coordination is a choice you make about how to organize the work. On the LST, coordination was survival. If one person lost their footing the space was small enough that the consequence landed on everyone. If one person's timing was off the motion of the deck amplified the error in ways that a stable floor would have absorbed. You became attuned to each other because the environment demanded it. You learned to anticipate not just the movement of the ship but the movement of the people working alongside you, because the ship moved all of you simultaneously and the only way to maintain output was to move together rather than each independently.

The nights at sea were unlike anything the land had offered.

Away from the base and away from the ports, away from city light and institutional noise, the ocean at night opened a sky that had no competition. The Pacific is vast in a way that maps do not communicate. Standing on the deck of a ship in the middle of it, you understand the vastness not as information but as presence. The horizon in every direction. No land. No reference point that belongs to the human world. Just water and sky and the particular silence of a place that has been operating on its own logic for longer than any institution or any person or any war.

I looked up on those nights.

I had looked up at the sky before. The desert had given me that habit. But the desert sky and the Pacific sky were different experiences of the same infinite. The desert stripped the ground away and left the sky. The ocean stripped everything away and left the sky and the water and a silence so complete that the stars felt close in a way they had not felt on land.

I did not know Orion yet.

I did not have a name for what I was looking at or a framework for understanding what the patterns above me meant or a language for the particular feeling of looking up at something that enormous and feeling something other than small.

But I looked.

Night after night, when the watch was done and the kitchen had been secured and the ship was moving through the dark Pacific on its own schedule, I looked up.

The stars were there.

Not yet named. Not yet connected to anything I understood. But present in the way that things are present before you have language for them, before meaning has been assigned, before the experience has been organized into something the mind can hold.

The ocean planted something the desert would later name.

And I carried it forward without knowing what I was carrying.

The WESTPAC deployment was many things before it was anything I could describe. It was the first time the world had been larger than the institution. The first time I had operated in an environment that the Marine Corps had sent me to but could not fully prepare me for. The first time I had cooked under conditions that required not the application of a standard but the adaptation of everything I had learned to circumstances the standard had not anticipated.

Moving with it rather than fighting it.

That was the education.

Not just of the ship.

Of everything that was coming.

CHAPTER 14

WestPac — The World

I had heard all the stories long before we ever left.

Everyone had. Stories passed down by guys who had already been out there, who had made the circuit and come back with the particular authority of people who had been somewhere you had not. Stories sharpened with each retelling. Stories about ports and cities and nights that didn't end the way nights back home ended. Stories about being young and far from home and suddenly standing in a world that was nothing like the one you had grown up inside of.

By the time the orders came I thought I knew what WESTPAC was.

I didn't.

What I encountered wasn't the world the stories promised. It was bigger. Louder. Less impressed with me. The world didn't open its arms toward a young Marine from St. Louis who had never been outside the United States. It moved past us at full speed, entirely indifferent to our expectation that it would pause long enough to be understood.

That was the first lesson.

Korea. Hong Kong. Singapore. Malaysia. Philippines.

Each place had its own rhythm. Its own particular way of organizing the hours and the people and the exchange between strangers. Its own set of rules that operated independently of whether you knew what they were. Its own understanding of what mattered and what didn't and how much of each thing a person needed to live a life that felt complete.

None of those understandings matched the one I had arrived with.

Leather in Korea. The market stalls, the particular smell of worked hide, the vendors who read your interest before you had expressed it and adjusted their presentation accordingly. Electronics in Hong Kong, a density of goods and commerce that made the American version of abundance feel modest by comparison. Silk in Malaysia, a texture and a color palette that had no equivalent in anything I had handled before.

But what stayed with me wasn't what we bought.

It was what we saw.

Cobra Gold made that clear before we reached any of the ports.

It wasn't a training exercise the way I had imagined training exercises. It was scale. Nations layered on top of one another. Languages and uniforms and command structures overlapping in ways that didn't always align and didn't always produce the coordination they were designed to produce. Live-fire training that felt real enough to remind you that mistakes didn't need an enemy to be fatal.

Death occurred around us during Cobra Gold.

Not dramatically. Not with the ceremony that the word carries in movies or in the stories told at bars. Accidents. Training incidents. Bodies that didn't get back up. Moments where everything stopped just long enough to acknowledge that someone was gone and then started again without that person.

No speeches.

No hero framing.

Just absence.

Death didn't wait for combat. It existed wherever complexity met motion and attention slipped for a moment too long. That was the second lesson.

Boy meets world.

And the world does not explain itself.

We moved through the ports afterward with different eyes. The stories we had heard didn't vanish, they just lost authority. The world wasn't dangerous in the ways the stories had described. It was dangerous in quieter, less cinematic ways. Unpredictable. Indifferent. Unimpressed by the particular confidence of people who had arrived assuming the rules would be familiar.

I realized quickly how small I was.

Not insignificant. Small.

The difference mattered more than I could articulate at the time. Back home in St. Louis, back on base at Camp Pendleton, the world had been arranged around systems I understood. The hierarchy of the Corps. The geography of the neighborhood. The particular social logic of environments I had grown up inside and learned to navigate. Here nothing bent toward me. If I wanted to understand anything I had to watch first. Learn before acting. Move without assuming the rules were the same.

That awareness didn't arrive as fear.

It arrived as humility.

And humility, for a Marine trained to project confidence and occupy space with authority, was a specific and unfamiliar education.

How people lived.

How they moved.

How they valued things differently.

Those three observations from the source material deserve to be unpacked because each one contained a complete lesson.

How people lived meant the physical arrangement of daily life in the places we passed through. The density of the markets in Hong Kong, where commerce and residence occupied the same vertical space in ways that American urban planning had never produced. The rhythm of the streets in Malaysia, where the pace of movement was different from the institutional urgency that governed everything on base. The particular relationship between neighbors in the Philippines, which I would understand more fully one day very soon in a courtyard I had not yet entered.

What I observed was that there were ways of organizing a life that produced dignity and community without requiring the material scale that America had taught me to associate with both. People who had less, measured by every metric the culture I came from used to measure, who nonetheless moved through their days with a completeness that the abundance I had come from did not guarantee.

How they moved meant the body language of people operating inside systems built by and for themselves. Not the body language of deference or the performance of welcome that tourism produces. The natural movement of people in their own environment, unhurried, unperformed, not organized around the presence of young American servicemen who were passing through.

We were visitors. Not guests. There is a difference. Guests are invited and expected and accommodated. Visitors arrive and the world continues without reorganizing itself around their presence.

The world kept moving. Whether we were ready or not.

How they valued things differently meant the particular recalibration that happened when I encountered people for whom the American version of more was not the aspiration. Not because they lacked ambition or because poverty had trained them to accept less. Because the hierarchy of value they operated inside was organized differently. Community over acquisition. Relationship over transaction. Presence over production.

These observations did not arrive as fully formed insights in the moment. They arrived as images. As sensory memories. As the specific texture of moments that lodged themselves in a way that generic experience does not and that would only reveal their full meaning years later when I had language for what I had been shown.

At night, sound changed.

Away from the base and the ship, in the streets and the markets and the spaces where the ports opened into the lives of the people who lived in them, music found us. Not the music I had grown up with. Rhythms I hadn't grown up with. Beats built on repetition instead of melody. Patterns that looped and layered rather than resolving toward a conclusion.

House music.

I didn't know what it was called yet. I only knew that it didn't build toward release the way the music I knew built toward release. It didn't tell a story with a beginning and an end. It pressed forward. It looped. It existed in the present tense without apology or explanation, consistent and unbothered by interpretation.

Something in that structure matched what the ports had already been teaching me.

Pattern without resolution.

Presence without destination.

The world keeps moving and the music keeps moving and neither of them pauses to explain themselves to the people passing through.

That sound stayed with me the way few things from WESTPAC stayed with me. Not as a memory exactly. As a texture. A quality of experience that I would recognize years later when the same music found me again in a different context and I would understand, in retrospect, that my body had been absorbing its logic long before my mind had a name for what it was absorbing.

The repetition wasn't boring.

It was stabilizing.

A steady pulse you could orient to when everything else was unanchored. A structure that existed independently of whether you understood it or approved of it or felt prepared for it.

By the time we had moved through the circuit of WESTPAC, through Cobra Gold and the ports and the markets and the nights of unfamiliar music, the stories that had preceded the deployment had lost whatever authority they had carried. Not because they were false. Because they were incomplete. They had described the surface of the experience without accounting for what the experience actually cost and produced.

What I carried back from those ports wasn't thrill.

It was orientation.

The understanding that the world does not operate by familiar rules. That confidence without awareness gets you into trouble. That humility is not weakness but the necessary precondition for learning anything real from an environment that owes you nothing.

And underneath all of it, quieter than any of the specific lessons, the growing recognition that the way my country had taught me to understand abundance and respect and what a full life required was not the only understanding available.

I had not yet sat in the courtyard.

I had not yet heard the words that would make this implicit understanding explicit.

But the ground was being prepared.

And the world, indifferent and unhurried and entirely unimpressed, was doing the preparing.

CHAPTER 15

The Courtyard

There are moments that do not announce their importance at the time they happen.

They arrive without ceremony. They fit into the flow of a day that is already full of other things. You are in a place you have not been before, moving through the particular combination of curiosity and caution that travel in unfamiliar environments produces, and then something happens that is so simple and so complete that the mind does not immediately know how to categorize it. It is too small to be called an event. It is too significant to be dismissed as ordinary. It settles somewhere in the body and waits, patient as everything that is true, for the understanding to arrive.

The Courtyard arrived that way.

We were in the Philippines.

The specifics of how we came to be there, which port, which street, which sequence of movement through the neighborhood, have blurred with time the way the edges of things blur when the center of them remains perfectly clear. What I remember is the apartment complex. Small. The kind of building that houses people who are not rich and have not built their lives around the expectation of becoming rich. Functional. Dense. Organized around the courtyard at its center the way a community is organized around the thing that holds it together.

We brought one plate of food.

Not a feast. Not a gesture designed to impress or to demonstrate generosity on a scale that would be noticed and remembered. One plate. The kind of contribution that could be made without calculation or ceremony, offered into a situation without knowing exactly what the situation would do with it.

What the situation did with it was not what I expected.

Everyone came down.

The people who lived in that building, residents whose lives had nothing to do with the military ships in the harbor or the young American servicemen moving through their neighborhood, came down into the courtyard. Not because they had been summoned. Not because any announcement had been made. Because one plate of food had appeared in the shared space and the shared space was for everyone and what was in it belonged to everyone by the simple logic of belonging.

They sat in a circle.

The circle matters. Not a line. Not a table with a head and a foot and a hierarchy of proximity to whoever was serving. A circle, which has no head and no foot, no position of greater or lesser access, no arrangement that places any person closer to the resource than any other. Everyone in the circle occupied the same relationship to what was being shared.

And they shared.

No hesitation.

That phrase is the one that lodged itself deepest and has stayed with me longest. Not the sharing itself, though the sharing was remarkable by the standards of every environment I had been living inside. The absence of hesitation. The particular quality of a community that moved toward sharing so naturally and so immediately that the pause between the plate arriving and the sharing beginning was too short to measure.

In every environment I had grown up in and trained in and operated inside, sharing required calculation.

Is there enough? Who has priority? What do I keep for myself? What is owed to me before I give to others? These questions were not always conscious. They were structural, built into the logic of the environments I knew, which were organized around the assumption that resources were finite and that the individual's relationship to finite resources was competitive by nature.

The courtyard did not operate on that logic.

Either everyone ate.

Or no one ate.

Those six words contained a complete philosophy of community. Not the philosophy of a text or a tradition or a formal teaching. The practical, lived philosophy of people whose relationship with scarcity had taught them something about abundance that abundance itself had not taught me.

When there is not enough for everyone, there is not enough for anyone.

When there is enough for anyone, it is enough for everyone.

The circle does not divide. It distributes.

I sat in that courtyard as someone who had been trained, from the first day of service, to hold a position. To secure a perimeter. To know where my resources were and to account for them and to protect them from the conditions that might deplete them. The military kitchen had refined this instinct into professional precision. Everything in its place. Mise en place. Controlled production. Measured output. The standard maintained through the careful management of everything that went into it.

All of that was still true and all of it still mattered.

But it had been organized around a different center than the one I was sitting inside now.

The center of everything I had learned was the individual holding the standard. The individual maintaining the output. The individual taking responsibility for their portion of the operation and executing it with the precision the standard required.

The center of this courtyard was the circle.

Not the individual within it. The circle itself. The shared space that existed because everyone had agreed, without the agreement needing to be stated, that the space was shared. That what arrived in it belonged to it. That belonging to the circle meant belonging to each other in the specific and practical sense that when one person had something everyone had it and when one person had nothing the something that others had was incomplete until it was shared.

One plate.

Distributed.

Without hesitation.

I thought about the kitchens I had worked in. The 1,200 Marines at Camp Horno. The 3,000 at San Onofre. The particular professional satisfaction of feeding that volume with consistency and precision and the internalized standard that Overton had given a name to.

I had been feeding people.

But I had been feeding them as individuals moving through a line. As units of a mass that had a daily caloric requirement that the kitchen was responsible for meeting. As the downstream recipients of a production process that was organized around output rather than around them.

The courtyard showed me something the kitchen had not shown me yet.

Food is not only fuel.

It is the physical expression of a community's relationship with itself. The act of sharing it is the act of acknowledging that the people around you matter in a way that is prior to transaction and prior to obligation and prior to the calculation of what is owed and what is kept. The circle in that courtyard was not performing generosity. It was simply being what it was, a community, for whom sharing was not a virtue to be demonstrated but a condition of existence to be honored.

That distinction would take years to fully surface.

The seed planted in that courtyard would grow slowly and with patience into something that would define not just how I cooked but what I believed cooking was for. The professional life that would follow the Marine Corps, the kitchens and the restaurants and the ventures and the Orion that would become the name for all of it, would carry this moment underneath, not always visible, not always named, but present.

Present the way Orion had been present over the Pacific before I had a name for it.

Before the meaning had been assigned.

But real.

And working.

The plate was finished.

Everyone had eaten.

The circle dispersed back into the building and the building dispersed back into the neighborhood and the neighborhood dispersed back into the city and the city continued on its own schedule as it had before we arrived and would after we left.

The world, as Chapter 14 had observed, does not pause to explain itself.

But sometimes, if you are present enough and quiet enough and humble enough to receive what it is offering rather than what you came expecting, it shows you something.

The courtyard showed me something.

Not a lesson I could have articulated on the walk back to the ship. Not an insight I wrote down or shared with anyone or processed into language that evening.

Just a circle.

Just a plate.

Just the unhesitating movement of a community toward what it needed to be.

And the particular stillness of a young man from St. Louis sitting inside it, feeling something, he did not yet have words for, carrying it forward without knowing what he was carrying.

Either everyone ate.

Or no one ate.

That stayed with me.

CHAPTER 16

Respect vs More

The question came from a genuine place.

That is important to understand before anything else about this conversation. The question was not asked with malice or condescension or the particular arrogance that sometimes accompanies the assumption that the questioner's world is the world everyone else aspires to enter. It was asked the way young people ask questions when they are standing in a place that is not their own and trying to build a bridge between what they know and what they are seeing.

Wouldn't you want to come to America?

It was the question of someone who had grown up inside the story America tells about itself. The story of abundance and opportunity and the particular gravity of a country that had been presented, in every classroom and every news broadcast and every casual assumption of the culture that produced it, as the destination. The place everyone else was trying to reach. The standard against which other ways of living were measured and found wanting.

I had grown up inside that story too.

I had worn its uniform. I was carrying its rifle. I had committed years of my life to its service without questioning the fundamental premise that what I was serving was the best version of what a country could be, and that the rest of the world, given the choice, would choose to be where I was from.

She didn't hesitate.

That is the detail that has stayed with me longer than any other detail of that conversation. Not the words themselves, though the words were precise and true and unanswerable. The absence of hesitation. The same quality the courtyard had shown me, the movement toward truth without the pause of calculation, without the softening that politeness or deference or the desire to avoid offense might have produced.

She had already thought about this.

She had already formed her view, from her position in the world, looking at Americans who arrived in her country with the confidence of people who had never been required to question whether their confidence was earned, and she had arrived at an understanding that was clear enough to deliver without preparation.

You are not respected in your own country.

Six words.

I want to sit with them the way they sat with me when they landed, because they deserve that. They deserve more than the quick acknowledgment that they were true and the equally quick movement past them that discomfort can produce in a person who is not ready to fully receive what is being offered.

She was not talking about general respect. She was not making a philosophical observation about the nature of American culture. She was looking at me. At a young man from St. Louis, American Indian Cherokee and Blackfoot and Chickasaw, wearing the uniform of a country that had specific and documented and unrectified relationships with the people that uniform represented. A country that had taken land and taken language and taken children and taken the particular continuity of culture that makes a people whole, and had offered in return exactly what she named.

More.

More goods. More access. More material scale. More of the measurable things that the story America tells about itself uses to define quality of life.

Not respect.

More.

That distinction is not abstract.

It is the difference between being seen and being fed. Between being acknowledged as someone whose presence in the world carries inherent worth that exists prior to any transaction and being provided for in ways that meet the body's requirements without addressing the soul's. Between the courtyard and the mess hall line. Between the circle and the queue.

That landed.

The word in the original source is exactly right. Landed. Not arrived. Not was received. Landed. The way something lands when it comes from height and makes contact with solid ground and the impact is felt in the body before the mind has processed what happened. The way truth lands when it is delivered without softening by someone who is not performing it but simply stating it.

We had more.

I had grown up knowing that. Had been taught to be grateful for it. Had absorbed the implicit argument that more was the evidence of better, that the scale of American abundance was the proof of

American rightness, that the people who had less had less because they had not yet arrived at where America had arrived and that arriving was the aspiration that should organize everything.

But more didn't mean better.

I knew that too; in the way you know things that the culture has not yet given you permission to say. The courtyard had shown it to me the day before, or the week before, or whenever it was in the sequence of WESTPAC that I had sat in that circle and watched one plate become enough for everyone without anyone pausing to calculate whether it was enough for them. The courtyard had shown me that community organized around sharing produced something that abundance organized around the individual could not purchase.

She had given me the language for what the courtyard had shown.

Not more. Respect.

Respect is the acknowledgment that a person's existence has value that precedes their utility. That they are not only worth what they can produce or what they can contribute to the system they live inside. That their history and their heritage and the particular way they carry themselves through the world matters independently of whether that mattering is convenient for the people around them.

She saw me as someone whose country had not given him that.

And she was not wrong.

The particular complexity of being American Indian in the uniform of the American military is not something I had been given language for before that conversation. The Corps had given me identity. It had given me discipline and standard and the particular pride of belonging to something that demanded everything you had. It had given me, through Overton and the kitchens and the standard, a sense of what earned pride felt like.

But it had not given me the framework to sit with what she was saying.

The framework came later. In pieces. Over years. Through the particular education of a life that has had to hold complexity without resolving it, that has had to carry pride in service alongside grief for what service has meant historically for people who look like me, that has had to find the thread of dignity that runs through both without pretending either one cancels the other.

In that moment I only had the landing.

The weight of something true arriving in the body without the mind being fully prepared to receive it.

We had more.

She had respect.

She had looked at the abundance and the confidence and the assumption that arrival in America was the aspiration everyone shared and she had offered a different accounting. Not with anger. Not with the agenda of someone trying to wound or diminish. With the particular clarity of a person who had examined the question honestly and arrived at an honest answer.

And she had delivered it without hesitation.

Because hesitation is what you add when you are not sure of the truth or not sure you have the right to speak it. She was sure of both.

I did not have a response.

That absence is also worth naming. In most conversations, the absence of a response would be a failure. A loss. A sign that the other person's argument had prevailed and that the correct thing to do was to recover as quickly as possible and return to a defensible position.

This was not most conversations.

This was a moment where the absence of a response was the most honest thing available. Where the thing to do was not to argue or to defend or to explain the complexity of a relationship with a country that is genuinely complex. Where the thing to do was to receive what had been given and carry it forward and let it do the work that truth does when it is not argued away.

I carried it.

Through the rest of WESTPAC. Through the return to Camp Pendleton. Through the preparation for war. Through the desert and the return and the years that followed. I carried it the way I had learned on the ship to carry things in motion, not fighting it, not trying to set it down and move on unencumbered, but moving with it, adjusting to its weight, letting it be part of the load rather than something extra that needed to be resolved before I could continue.

Respect mattered more.

That is the closing line of the original and it is the right closing line because it is not a conclusion. It is a reorientation. A shift in the hierarchy of what matters that would quietly rearrange itself into everything that followed. Into how I led. Into what I built. Into the particular kind of table I would try to create in the culinary life that waited on the other side of the uniform, where the goal was not to produce output for people moving through a line but to create a space where people felt what the courtyard had shown me was possible.

Seen.

Fed.

Respected.

Not because they had earned it through performance or compliance or the demonstration of values someone else had decided were worth rewarding.

Because they were there.

And being there was enough.

Respect mattered more.

She had said it without hesitation.

And it has never stopped being true.

CHAPTER 17

The Return Across Hawaii

The Pacific is not a small thing to cross.

It takes time in a way that air travel has made it easy to forget. When you move through it on a ship rather than above it in a pressurized cabin where the ocean is reduced to a blue abstraction visible through a small oval window, you feel its scale in your body. Days pass. The horizon is always the same distance away. The water does not change regardless of how far you move across it. It simply continues, vast and indifferent and organized according to a logic that has nothing to do with human schedules or human urgency.

We had been out there for months.

Moving through the ports and the training exercises and the particular education of WESTPAC, absorbing what the world had offered to a young man from St. Louis who had arrived with a set of assumptions and was returning with a different set of questions. The ship had taught adaptation. The ports had taught humility. The courtyard had shown what sharing without hesitation looked like. The woman had said what no one at home had said.

All of it was in the body now.

Not yet organized into language or understanding that could be articulated or explained. In the body, the way the most durable learning always arrives. Carried without being held consciously. Present without being named.

The return journey moved through Hawaii.

And something changed.

The pace slowed.

That is not a small thing in a context that had been defined by forward motion, by the particular rhythm of a deployment that moved continuously, that arrived and departed and processed and produced and never fully paused long enough to allow the accumulated experience to settle into anything resembling stillness. The Marine Corps generates momentum. It organizes its people around movement and mission and the constant forward orientation of people who have been trained to treat stillness as vulnerability.

Hawaii slowed that momentum.

Not by design. Not as a formal decompression or a deliberate transition ritual. Simply by being what it was. A place that operated at a different pace than the operational tempo we had been living inside. A place where the air was warm and fragrant and the landscape was lush in a way that the Pacific ports and the ship and the training environments had not been. A place that was American in its affiliation but not American in its feeling, not the America of bases and formations and the institutional rhythms that had organized most of my experience of being American in uniform.

Something in the body recognized the permission to slow down.

Not to stop. Not to release the readiness that had become structural at this point, that lived in the posture and the eyes and the particular quality of attention that WESTPAC had refined from the foundation the desert would later sharpen into something harder and more permanent. But to slow. To let the pace of the environment inform the pace of movement rather than overriding it with the institutional urgency that the Corps produced in every context it controlled.

Music played.

Reggae had been in the ports beforc, threading through the streets of the Philippines and the markets of Malaysia, part of the sonic landscape of the Pacific that had introduced itself to a young Marine who had grown up on different rhythms and different resolutions. But in Hawaii it felt different. Less peripheral. More present. Reggae carries a particular relationship with time, a refusal of urgency, a deep rootedness in the present moment that does not lean forward into what is coming or backward into what has passed. It exists in the now with the complete ease of something that has already made its peace with the world.

House music had been following us since the ports too, the beats built on repetition, the patterns that looped and layered without resolving, the particular structure that had felt stabilizing in the way that consistency feels stabilizing when everything else is in motion. Both of them together in Hawaii produced something the individual forms could not produce alone. A space. A quality of time that was unhurried without being empty. Present without being demanding.

For a few days, or however long the return across Hawaii lasted, something that resembled peace was available.

Not the peace of resolution. Nothing had been resolved. The woman's words were still sitting in the body unrectified. The courtyard was still planted, not yet grown into anything with a name. The months of motion and exposure and the particular education of having the world be larger than the story you were given about it were all present, all still being absorbed, all still waiting for the distancc and the time that processing requires.

But the pace had slowed.

And in that slowing, something became briefly visible that the forward motion had kept hidden.

How much had been taken in.

How much was being carried.

How different the person making the return crossing was from the person who had made the outbound one.

I did not inventory this consciously. I did not sit down and account for what WESTPAC had produced or catalog the lessons or try to understand what I was bringing back that I had not taken out. It was not that kind of awareness. It was the body's awareness. The particular quality of presence that stillness allows when the stillness is genuine, when the pacc has actually slowed enough for the accumulated weight of experience to be felt rather than simply carried.

The music played.

The ocean moved.

The sky over Hawaii was the same sky that had been over the Pacific for the entire deployment, the same sky I had looked up at from the deck of the LST on nights when the stars were out and the horizon was gone and the universe felt close in the particular way it feels close when there is nothing between you and it. The same sky I had not yet learned to read but had already begun to love, had already begun to rely on in the way Joseph would later understand reliance as something sturdier than belief.

Those stars were there.

Still unnamed.

Still present.

Still working.

Then the word came.

It did not arrive with drama, It did not interrupt the music with an alarm or a formal announcement or the kind of ceremony that the gravity of the information might seem to require. It came the way institutional information always comes, through the chain of command, in language that was measured and official and organized around the operational requirements of the news it was delivering rather than around the human experience of receiving it.

The Gulf was heating up.

War was coming.

The particular stillness that Hawaii had offered, the slowing of pace and the music and the briefly available quality of something that was not quite peace but was close enough to peace to be felt as relief, contracted.

Not immediately. Not with the sudden violence of a door slamming. More like a temperature change. The warmth that had been present in the air was still technically present but was no longer the dominant condition. Something else had entered the environment and had reorganized what everything else meant.

The music kept playing.

But it no longer reached the place where I was standing.

Not because it stopped. Because the place where I was standing had moved. The person listening to it was already somewhere else, already recalibrating, already processing what the word meant and what it required and what the body would need to be in order to meet what was coming.

Everything shifted again.

That phrase is the right phrase because shift is the right word. Not collapse. Not fear, though fear was present in the way fear is always present when the information that arrives is the information you cannot take back. Shift. The particular internal reorganization that happens when the context changes and everything you have been carrying reorients itself around the new center of gravity.

WESTPAC had been formation.

The ship had taught adaptation. The ports had taught humility. The courtyard had shown community. The woman had given truth. Hawaii had offered, briefly, the space to feel what all of it had produced.

And now the context was changing.

What had been formation was about to become application.

Everything WESTPAC had built, every lesson absorbed through the ports and the courtyard and the nights of unfamiliar music and the particular education of having the world be larger than expected, was about to be tested in an environment that had none of the generosity of the Pacific. An environment where the stakes were not the stakes of a young man learning what he did not know. The stakes of a Marine in a war zone where what he knew and what he had become would be required in full.

The music played.

The ocean moved.

The stars were out somewhere above the clouds.

And the word had been given.

War was coming.

Everything had already shifted by the time the sentence finished.

Not because of fear.

Because that is what it means to be trained for something. When the thing arrives, the body does not wait for the mind to process the implications. It moves. It orients. It prepares. It becomes what it has been becoming since the first watch in the desert and the first 2 a.m. kitchen and the first time a standard was held not because someone was watching but because the standard was the standard and the person holding it had decided, quietly and without ceremony, that it was theirs.

The formation was complete.

The application was beginning.

Part III ends here.

Part IV begins in the shadow of what is coming.

PART IV: TARGETED

CHAPTER 18

Return to Horno

We returned from WESTPAC changed, whether we knew it or not.

That is the honest starting point. Not that we came back the same people who had left and were simply returning to a familiar environment. Not that the months of the Pacific, the ship and the ports and the courtyard and the woman's words and the music and the particular education of having the world be larger than the story given about it, had passed through us without leaving a mark.

They had left a mark.

The world had expanded.

The rhythm of ports, people, and possibility still lived in the body the way things live in the body when they have been absorbed rather than simply experienced. Not as memories that required conscious retrieval. As a changed quality of attention. A different relationship with assumption. A wider peripheral vision, not physical but psychological, the awareness that the frame you had been operating inside was not the only frame available and that other frames existed and produced different understandings of the same world.

That was what came back with us.

Not just people. Changed people.

But the base had not changed.

Camp Horno was exactly as it had been. The same buildings. The same hierarchy. The same institutional rhythms. The same expectations organized around the same systems that had been in place before WESTPAC, that would be in place after WESTPAC, that the deployment had not been designed to challenge or expand or reconsider.

The institution does not go on WESTPAC.

The people do.

And the people who return are not always the same shape as the space that was kept for them.

Coming back wasn't the same.

That observation sounds simple and it is not simple at all. Coming back means the reunion of a changed interior with an unchanged exterior. It means the person who absorbed the courtyard and the woman's words and the nights of unfamiliar music over the Pacific now has to operate inside an environment that has no framework for any of that. That treats the months away as operational experience rather than as the personal and philosophical education it had also been. That expects the returning Marine to re-enter the institution at the point he left it, as if the leaving had not produced anything that needed to be accounted for.

The energy was tighter.

Not hostile. Not aggressive. Tight in the way that an environment gets tight when it is processing information it has not yet organized into something it can communicate. When decisions are being made above the level that most people can see. When the shape of something large is forming in the background and everyone can feel its pressure without being able to see its form.

More tension.

The Gulf was heating up.

That was the information moving through the base in the weeks after our return. Not as official communication. Not as briefings or formal updates through the chain of command. As the particular sideways movement of information that institutions produce when the information is real and consequential and not yet ready to be stated officially. Conversations that quieted when the wrong person walked into the room. Looks exchanged between people who knew more than they were saying. The particular quality of attention that a community develops when it is collectively aware that something is coming without being collectively told what it is.

Information moved sideways instead of forward.

Rumors passed between ranks. News fragments. Names floated casually, then more deliberately. Different words for the same thing: something was happening in the Gulf and the Marine Corps was going to be involved and the question of who was going to be involved and in what capacity was being answered somewhere above the deck plates in ways that had not yet arrived at the level where most of us were standing.

I was aware of it the way you are aware of weather.

Not as a specific threat I could identify and address. As a change in atmospheric pressure. The environment registering something that the conscious mind had not yet been given enough information to name. The same quality of awareness that the watch had built in Chapter 2, the capacity to register deviation before deviation had fully formed, now operating in the social and institutional environment of Camp Horno the way it had operated in the desert darkness.

Something was forming.

I hadn't changed.

But how I was received had.

That asymmetry is worth sitting with because it is one of the most disorienting experiences a person can have. You are the same person. You have the same history, the same demonstrated capabilities, the same record that had earned the E-6 billet at three grades below its rank requirement. Nothing about you has diminished. If anything, WESTPAC has added to what you are carrying. The world is larger. The understanding is deeper. The particular humility that the Pacific had installed sits underneath everything with a quiet authority that nothing in the pre-WESTPAC version of yourself had possessed.

And the environment receives all of that differently than it received you before.

Not with hostility. Not with a formal change in status or a documented shift in how you were regarded. With a quality of distance that is almost imperceptible until you have the particular sensitivity that the watch trained into you. The way a room slightly reorganizes itself around the presence of someone it is in the process of deciding something about. The way conversations adjust their edges when a specific person enters them. The way the air carries information that has not yet been said and may never be said directly but is nonetheless present and being communicated and received.

That shift mattered.

Not because of what it felt like in the moment. Because of what it indicated. A man who had learned to read terrain, to look for the deviation before it became a problem, to track the pattern before it produced a consequence, did not dismiss what he was feeling in the social terrain of Camp Horno after WESTPAC.

He read it.

He did not know yet what the reading meant or where it was pointing. He knew that the environment had changed in a way that the environment was not yet explaining. He knew that information was moving sideways instead of forward and that when information moves sideways instead of forward it is because someone above you has already made a decision about you and the decision has not yet arrived.

He knew that something was coming.

He stayed ready.

Not out of paranoia. Not out of fear. Out of the same discipline that had been present since the first watch in the dark, since the 2 a.m. kitchen, since the sixteen ovens and the 2,880 strips of bacon and the particular education of a man who had learned to hold the full picture in awareness without losing any part of it.

The Gulf was heating up.

And Camp Horno, unchanged and institutional and organized around the same rhythms it had always been organized around, was quietly deciding something that had not yet been announced.

Joseph Randall was on that list.

He did not know it yet.

He felt it the way you feel weather before it arrives.

In the pressure.

In the silence between what was being said and what was actually true.

In the particular quality of a return that did not feel like a return at all.

CHAPTER 19

The List

It began as information without shape.

The way most consequential things begin. Not with an announcement or a formal notification or the kind of official communication that gives you something to respond to. With the particular quality of institutional atmosphere that Chapter 18 described. Conversations quieting at the wrong moments. Information moving sideways instead of forward. The awareness of something forming above the level where you were standing, visible only through its pressure, through the way the air in a room change when decisions have already been made that the room has not yet been told about.

We were told that some Marines would be reassigned to other units.

Nothing official.

Nothing explained.

Just the statement, delivered without elaboration, that the institution was moving some of its people and that the criteria for who would be moved and who would remain had not been communicated and would not be communicated in any form that invited discussion or question or appeal.

I wasn't worried.

Not because I had information that should have reassured me. Because I had a position in the logic of the situation that seemed, by every rational measure, to protect me from what was being described. I had juniors. Marines below me in rank and tenure who would, in any system organized around the principles of seniority and demonstrated excellence that the Corps nominally operated by, be the first candidates for reassignment. That is how it was supposed to work. The most junior go first. The ones who have demonstrated the most go last, or not at all.

I had earned my position.

The E-6 billet. The best mess hall on Camp Pendleton. The standard Overton had given and that I had carried forward and extended into sixteen Marines who now held it themselves. The particular record of a man who had done more than the rank on his collar said he was supposed to do and had done it without complaint and without seeking acknowledgment and with the full internalized commitment to the standard that Chapters 7 through 12 had been building toward.

By rank alone, I should have been safe.

But the Marines don't always move on merit.

That sentence needs to be read carefully because it is not a complaint. It is not the bitterness of a man who failed to receive what he was owed and is accounting for the deficit. It is an observation about the nature of institutions, which are built by and operated by people, and people bring to their positions within institutions all the things that people bring everywhere. Not just merit and principle and the honest assessment of demonstrated capability. Also politics. Also convenience. Also the decisions made far above the deck plates by people who have information and motivations that the people below them cannot see and are not given access to.

Sometimes they move on politics.

Sometimes they move on convenience.

Sometimes they move on decisions made far above the deck plates.

A list appeared.

Eight names.

Mine was on it.

That fact registered with a particular quality of stillness. Not panic. Not the flood of emotion that the news might have been expected to produce in a younger man or a man who had not been trained in the discipline of receiving information without letting the information move him before he had assessed what it meant. The watch had built that. The 2 a.m. kitchen had built that. San Onofre and the sixteen ovens had built that. The particular capacity to hold something in awareness without immediately reacting to it, to let it be present while the full picture assembled itself.

Eight names.

One of them mine.

As days passed, the list grew smaller.

One name dropped.

Then another.

This is where the particular education of patience that the desert and the kitchen and the watch had built was tested in a way none of those environments had anticipated. Watching a list shrink is a specific and distinctive kind of waiting. Not the waiting of someone who does not know what is coming. The waiting of someone who can see exactly what is coming, can trace the direction of the movement, can calculate from the current trajectory exactly where it ends, and who must nonetheless continue to occupy the present moment, to execute the daily requirements of the position, to maintain the standard in the kitchen and the composure in the ranks and the professional bearing of someone who has not yet been officially told what has already been decided.

The list kept shrinking.

One name at a time.

Each dropped name was a small release for everyone whose name remained. A temporary loosening of the pressure. A moment of something that was not quite hope but was the recognition that the mathematics had shifted. That if the list needed to reach one and there were four names remaining, yours had only a one in four chance of being the one. Then one in three. Then one in two.

Then it was just me.

The morning of reassignment, we stood on the parade deck.

The same parade deck where Joseph had stood on April 8, 1991 and watched reunions unfold around him while he walked alone back to the barracks. The same physical space. A different kind of solitude.

By then the list had been reduced to one.

Mine.

I stood alone.

The others were released back to their units. They stepped out of the formation and back into the ordinary continuation of their service, the daily rhythm of the base; the particular relief of a man who had been on a list that shrinks and whose name had fallen off before the end. They returned to their kitchens and their routines and the version of their life that WESTPAC had interrupted and that could now resume.

I remained.

Waiting for orders that felt less like instructions and more like a verdict.

That distinction is exact. Instructions tell you what to do. A verdict tells you what has been decided about you. Instructions exist within a system where your participation matters, where your execution of the task is the point of the communication. A verdict exists within a system where the decision has already been made and the communication is simply the formal delivery of a conclusion that was never going to be different regardless of anything you might have said or done.

I wasn't reassigned because I failed.

I wasn't reassigned because I volunteered.

I was reassigned because I had been targeted.

Let those three sentences exist in the space they require before moving past them. Because they represent something that a man who had built everything on the principle that merit and standard and demonstrated excellence were the currencies that mattered needed time to process. Not process emotionally. Process structurally. To understand what kind of world he was actually operating inside and what that understanding required of him going forward.

The Marines don't always move on merit.

That was the lesson being delivered on the parade deck that morning. Not by a mentor who cared about his development. Not through the dignified accountability of the office where the Sergeants had made him do pushups and mentored him simultaneously and sent him out to flood the kitchen with soapy water. By the institution itself, operating according to its own logic, which was not always the logic it claimed to operate by.

Rank, which should have protected me, did the opposite.

I had been selected.

Sentenced.

That word is not an exaggeration. The title of the CANON source chapter is The Sentence. Because what happened on the parade deck that morning was not a reassignment in the operational sense. It was a sentencing in the human sense. A verdict delivered by a system that had decided something about a man and had no intention of explaining the reasoning because the reasoning was not the kind that survived explanation.

I stood on the parade deck.

The others were gone.

The orders arrived.

And Joseph Randall, who had earned the best mess hall on Camp Pendleton, who had run the E-6 billet three grades above his rank, who had stood with Overton's standard and held it without apology or compromise, who had carried the particular pride of a man who had done the work and earned the right to the position he occupied, received his verdict.

Las Pulgas.

The cannon cockers.

The sand before Christmas.

He accepted it the way a man accepts what cannot be changed.

Not with relief. Not with the false peace of someone who has convinced himself that the unjust thing is actually just. With the particular quality of acceptance that arrives when a man has fully understood the situation and has decided that the situation will not determine who he is or what he carries forward or what he becomes on the other side of it.

The institution had sentenced him.

It had not broken him.

It was not going to.

But the betrayal was real and it deserves to be named.

Not the reassignment itself. Reassignments happen. The Corps moves its people according to needs and decisions that individuals do not always have access to and that the institution does not always owe an explanation for. That is understood. That is the nature of service.

The betrayal was this: he was being sent to war.

Not with the unit he had built himself inside of. Not with the Marines he had stood next to and fed and led and whose quality he knew from years of shared work and shared standard and the particular intimacy of people who have been in each other's kitchens and on each other's watches and through each other's worst mornings. Not with the men whose faces he could read and whose instincts he trusted and who trusted his in return.

He was being sent as an unknown.

To a unit that did not know him.

Among men who had their own histories and their own bonds and their own understanding of who was reliable and who was not, built through the same kind of shared experience that he had built with the people he was being pulled away from.

In a combat environment, that matters more than almost anything else.

War is not fought by individuals. It is fought by people who know each other. Whose instincts are calibrated to each other. Who have already answered the question of whether the person next to them is someone they can count on when the margin is seven seconds and the choice is move or don't. That knowledge is not transferable. It is built through time and proximity and the particular education of having been through difficult things together and having emerged knowing something about each other that no introduction can produce.

He was being stripped of that.

Sent into the most dangerous environment a Marine can occupy as a stranger among strangers. A man whose name had just been reduced to the last one on a shrinking list arriving in a unit that had not asked for him and had not chosen him and would need time to assess him that the timeline of what was coming might not provide.

It was a death sentence dressed as a reassignment.

Not because Las Pulgas was a lesser unit. Because in war, the unknown is the most dangerous thing there is. And he was arriving unknown.

That was the full weight of what the parade deck delivered.

Not just the removal from the unit he had earned his place in. The particular vulnerability of being sent to face the most consequential thing in his life surrounded by people who did not yet know who he was or what he was capable of or whether he was someone worth standing next to when the alarms came.

He carried that.

He added it to everything else he was carrying.

And he walked off the parade deck.

He picked up his orders.

And he began to prepare for what was coming.

Not because the betrayal wasn't real.

Because what was coming was larger than the betrayal.

And because a man who had been built the way the preceding chapters had built him did not allow what had been done to him to determine what he was going to do.

The institution had sentenced him.

It had not defined him.

That distinction was going to matter in the sand.

CHAPTER 20

Pulgas

Las Pulgas.

Different base.

The orders had been clear on destination if not on anything else. Las Pulgas. The cannon cockers. The unit that would carry him into the sand before Christmas. Joseph Randall had been sentenced on the parade deck and the sentence had a specific address and a specific unit and a specific timeline and none of it had been delivered with apology or explanation or the acknowledgment that what was happening was anything other than routine institutional movement.

He moved.

Because that is what you do when the institution makes a decision about you. Not because you agree with the decision or because you have been persuaded that it is just. Because movement is the only option available that preserves what matters. Standing still in protest of a verdict that has already been rendered serves nothing except the comfort of the person standing still. Joseph Randall had not gotten this far by standing still.

He moved to Las Pulgas.

And Las Pulgas felt different immediately.

Different energy.

Not hostile. Not unwelcoming in any formal sense. Different the way environments feel different when you arrive in them already carrying something that the environment cannot see and cannot account for. He was a man who had just been sentenced, who had just stood alone on a parade deck while the others returned to their units, who was now present in a place he had not chosen and among people who had their own histories and their own relationships and their own understanding of what was coming that did not include him yet.

He stayed to himself.

That was not withdrawal. Not the retreat of a wounded man pulling away from the world to lick the wound privately. It was the specific economy of a man who understood that the moment he was in required conservation. That the energy available was finite and that the demands coming were going to be larger than anything that had come before and that spending what was available on the management of social dynamics in a new unit was a luxury the situation could not afford.

He observed instead.

Who moved with efficiency and who wasted motion. Who tracked the horizon and who stared at the ground. Who would be worth knowing when things went sideways. The same reading of human terrain that the watch had built and the kitchen had refined and WESTPAC had expanded, now applied to the men he would be moving into the desert with.

Packing.

Waiting.

Moving.

These three words from the original source deserve their full weight because they describe not just a physical process but a psychological one. Packing is the act of making the world portable. Of reducing everything that constitutes a life to what will fit in the space allowed and serve the purpose ahead. It is an act of radical prioritization. Everything that doesn't fit gets left behind. Everything that remains is what the situation has decided is essential.

Packing for war is different from every other kind of packing.

Because the question underneath every decision about what to take and what to leave is a question you do not ask directly. But it is present in the weight of every item considered and set aside or placed in the bag. The question of whether you will return for what you are leaving. Whether the life that is being reduced to its portable form will have the opportunity to expand again on the other side of whatever is coming.

You pack it anyway.

You pack it with the same precision you brought to the kitchen. Everything in its place. Everything with a purpose. No excess. No sentiment. What fits serves. What doesn't fit stays.

Waiting was the other education of Las Pulgas.

Waiting is not passive. Not for a man built the way the preceding chapters have built Joseph Randall. Waiting is the watch applied to time rather than to space. The sustained attention to a future that has not yet arrived, maintained at the same quality of presence that the four hours of desert darkness had required, that the 2 a.m. kitchen had required, that the sixteen ovens had required.

You stay ready.

Not by filling the waiting with noise or distraction or the particular coping mechanisms that waiting produces in people who have not been trained in thc discipline of stillness. By inhabiting the waiting fully. By being present in it without fighting it. Moving with it rather than against it the way the ship had taught him to move with the ocean rather than against it.

We were told we would be in the sand before Christmas.

As a concession, we were given Thanksgiving.

That word concession is exactly right and it is worth pausing on. A concession is something given by the party with power to the party without it. An acknowledgment that what is being required is large enough that something must be offered in return, not as compensation but as acknowledgment. The Marine Corps was going to send Joseph Randall to a war he had not volunteered for, in a unit he had not chosen, on a timeline that had not been negotiated. In exchange, it was giving him Thanksgiving.

He went home.

Home to St. Louis. To the house and the family and the world that had existed before the uniform. The world that the letters and the phone calls from the payphone had kept him connected to across the distance of the base and then across the distance of the Pacific and that had continued without him in the way that the lives of the people you love continue without you when you are somewhere they cannot follow.

My mother knew before I said anything.

Mothers always do.

Not because she had been told. Not because the institutional communication had reached her in a form she could read directly. Because a mother who has raised a child knows the quality of their presence when they walk through the door. Knows the difference between the ordinary weight a person carries and the specific weight of someone who has received information that has changed the texture of everything. She looked at her son and she knew.

She didn't ask him to explain it.

She didn't ask him to prepare her for it or soften it or deliver it in a form that would be easier to receive.

She knew.

And she responded the way she had always responded to the things that could not be changed. Not by pretending they were smaller than they were. Not by filling the space with reassurance that the space did not have room for. By honoring what was real with everything she had available to her.

She invited the entire family.

Cooked an extra-special Thanksgiving dinner.

That phrase, extra-special, is the most human phrase in the entire manuscript and it should be read with the full weight of what it contains. A mother who knew her son was going to war and who responded to that knowledge by cooking an extra-special Thanksgiving dinner. Not a larger dinner. Not a more expensive dinner. Extra-special. The particular quality of care and attention that a person who loves someone completely brings to the ordinary things when the ordinary things are all they have left to offer. When the situation is beyond their ability to change and what remains is the dignity of honoring it fully.

She fed her family.

She fed her son.

At the table, she sat me at the head.

That placement carries everything. In the Randall family table, that seat had a meaning that did not need to be explained to anyone sitting at it. The head of the table is where the person of honor sits. Where the person the family is gathered around sits. Where the person the meal is for sits.

She sat her son there.

Then she brought out a brass dinner bell.

She placed it in front of him and told him not to get up for anything.

If he needed something, he was to ring the bell.

That is the complete gesture of a mother honoring her son before sending him somewhere she cannot follow. Not with words that would be inadequate to what she felt. Not with the kind of emotional declaration that the moment might have seemed to require. With a brass dinner bell placed in front of the man she raised and the instruction that he was not to move from that seat for any reason, that she would come to him, that for the duration of this meal at this table in this house, everything he needed would be brought to him and nothing would be required of him except to receive it.

It was her way of honoring him.

It didn't change his situation.

It didn't alter the road ahead.

But it mattered.

He sat at the head of the table.

The family gathered around him.

The meal was served.

And for the duration of that Thanksgiving, Joseph Randall was not a Marine who had been sentenced to the sand. He was a son being honored by his mother in the only way she had left to honor him.

That mattered more than the situation could diminish.

Then the concession ended.

The orders remained.

Prior to boarding that plane, I had never been more scared in my entire life.

That sentence deserves to exist without immediate elaboration because it is the most honest sentence in the section and possibly in the book. Not the bravado of a man preparing for combat. Not the institutional confidence of a Marine who has been trained to project readiness regardless of internal state. The plain truth of a man who had been given Thanksgiving as a concession and was now standing at the departure gate of an experience he could not prepare for and could not avoid and would have done anything to not have to face.

I would have done anything not to go.

Twenty-two hours in the air.

The flight to a war zone is a specific and distinctive experience because it is the last extended period of time in which the thing you are traveling toward exists only as information and not yet as reality. The plane is still the world you know. The destination is still abstract. The twenty-two hours are the last hours of the person who has not yet been in a war, moving through the air toward the person who will have been.

Fear stayed through every phase.

Not the fear that paralyzes. The fear that is honest. The fear that a man feels when he has fully understood the situation he is entering and has not insulated himself from that understanding with false confidence or bravado or the performance of readiness that does not reach the place where the fear is sitting. The fear that sits with a man who has already made peace with the possibility of the worst outcome and has decided to go anyway.

That is the most honest fear available.

It stayed through every phase.

And then, somewhere in the final leg of the flight, something changed.

Not gradually. Not through a process of reasoning or reassurance or the slow accumulation of courage. Something in the body shifted. The same kind of shift that Chapter 4 had described as the system recognizing a new condition and reorganizing itself around it. The fear had been the appropriate response to information about a future that had not yet arrived. The future was now arriving. And the system, built across every chapter of this book, built by the watch and the kitchen and the sixteen ovens and the WESTPAC and the parade deck and the brass dinner bell, had reorganized itself around what was actually required.

Fear let go.

In its place came indifference.

Not the indifference of someone who does not care what happens. The indifference of someone who has already accepted every possible outcome and is no longer organizing their internal state around avoiding any of them. The particular freedom that arrives when a man has looked directly at the worst possibility and has decided that what he is and what he carries is enough to meet it.

Restraint dissolved.

The beast was released.

That beast had been building since Part I. Since the hypervigilance installed by the desert-trained sleep and the nightmares and the control that held everything in place. Since the standard that Overton had given and the discipline that San Onofre had refined and the promise made on the parade deck at Camp Pendleton that what the other Marines had released, he would contain. The beast was everything the formation had been containing. Everything the control had been holding in place. Everything that the years of structure and standard and discipline had been building toward without naming.

It did not need to be contained anymore.

There was no one to protect from it now.

There was only the desert ahead and the war that the desert contained and the particular application of everything the formation had produced.

There was no turning back.

Time for war.

The plane descended.

The formation was complete.

Part IV ends here and Part V begins in the sand.

PART V: WAR

CHAPTER 21

Arrival

The plane descended.

Twenty-two hours of fear had occupied the space between the world I had known and the world I was entering. Fear had stayed through every phase of the flight. Not the fear that paralyzes. The honest fear of someone who had fully understood what I was traveling toward and had not insulated himself from that understanding with false confidence or the performance of readiness that does not reach the place where the fear is sitting.

Then fear let go.

In its place, indifference. Restraint dissolved. The beast released.

The plane landed.

And the world that had been abstract for twenty-two hours became immediate in a way that no amount of preparation could have fully anticipated.

M16 in hand.

Gas mask ready.

No buildup.

No adjustment.

The institution that had given me Thanksgiving as a concession and twenty-two hours of air travel to cross from one version of my life to another was done making concessions. The sand was real. The air was wrong. The sky was not the sky.

Jets flew so low I could look up and read the writing on the missiles as they separated from the wings.

Not a news report. Not a briefing photograph. Standing on the ground in Saudi Arabia looking up at a military aircraft flying so low that the ordinance attached to its wings was legible. Letters and numbers stenciled on metal moving toward a destination where it would do what it had been built to do. That close. That real. That immediate.

The air smelled wrong.

Wrong is the exact word because wrong is what the nose communicates before the mind has identified the specific components of what it is processing. The brain registers threat through smell faster than through any other sense. The smell of burning oil. Of smoke that carried things in it that smoke in any previous environment had not carried. Of the particular combination of industrial combustion and something underneath it that the mind did not immediately name but the body recognized and responded to with a sharpening of every system.

Burning bodies.

Oil.

Smoke so thick it turned day into a permanent dusk.

The Kuwaiti oil fields were burning. The retreating Iraqi forces had set them ablaze in an act of destruction that was also a statement, a final assertion of damage in the face of defeat. The fires produced a smoke column that rose into the upper atmosphere and spread across the region like a second sky, a dark layer that sat above the actual sky and through which the sun existed somewhere unreachable.

We lived below the smoke line.

The sun existed somewhere above it.

Day was never fully day. There was light but it was the wrong color. Filtered through smoke. Dimmed and tinted and carrying in it the particular quality of illumination that exists when the light source has been modified by something it was not designed to pass through.

This was the environment.

Not a temporary condition we would adjust to. The environment. The air and the sky and the smell and the light that would define every day and every night for the duration of what was coming.

We were issued ammunition immediately.

Live rounds.

No ceremony.

That distinction from training is total. In training, ammunition is issued with procedure. With the formal acknowledgment that live rounds are different from blanks in ways that require the institution to mark the transition with protocol. Forms. Verification. The institutional recognition that the category of thing being handled has changed and that the change carries weight.

Here there was no ceremony because the ceremony was irrelevant. The rounds were live because the environment required live rounds and the environment was not interested in the institution's protocol for acknowledging that fact. You took them. You loaded. You moved.

Unapproved medication was handed out.

No labels anyone trusted.

Just instructions given once and not repeated.

You didn't ask questions.

The medication was to counter chemical attacks. The particular threat of chemical weapons in that theater had been briefed enough times that no one needed the briefing again. What had not been briefed, what no one was going to brief, was whether the medication being handed out had been fully tested, fully approved, fully understood in terms of what it would do to the body over time. You took it anyway. Because the alternative was not taking it and the alternative to not taking it was the reason the medication existed.

You didn't ask questions.

Sandbags were everywhere.

Being filled.

Being stacked.

Bunkers going up fast, like temporary thoughts meant to stop permanent consequences. The bunker is what you can build in the time available with the materials available. It is not permanent. It is not guaranteed. It is the best available answer to a threat that has no good answers. You fill the sandbags because filling sandbags is something you can do, and doing something is always better than standing in the open with nothing between you and what is coming.

First task: build.

Bunkers. Shelter.

Survival starts there.

Not with strategy or mission briefings or the higher architecture of the operational plan. With sandbags and entrenching tools and the physical work of building the simplest possible protection between your body and the environment that wants to end it.

We were assigned to a Howitzer unit.

Twenty clicks behind the front lines.

Close enough to feel the response without being close enough to see the impact. Inside the war but not at its edge. Close enough to know the war is real. Far enough to have a margin that the front lines did not have.

As the line advanced, so did we.

Always moving forward into the same danger from a different distance.

Familiar faces appeared sometimes.

Marines I hadn't seen since training. Since ships. Since another version of myself that existed before the smoke and the live rounds and the medication with no labels. We recognized each other quickly and the recognition passed quickly because nobody lingered in it. Lingering required a quality of present-tense ease that the environment did not offer. Recognition happened and then you moved because movement was what the situation required.

Food became a commodity.

I had spent Part II building the understanding that food was not just fuel, that the act of feeding people carried a dignity and a significance that the mere nutritional transaction did not account for. The courtyard had shown me that food was community. The woman had shown me that respect mattered more than more. And now food was a commodity.

Not because the people eating it had forgotten its deeper meaning. Because the environment had stripped everything to its functional layer. Food was what kept the body operational. The body being operational was what kept you alive. Keeping you alive was what allowed the mission to continue. The mission continuing was the point of everything the institution was doing in this sand.

Food as commodity was not a lesser thing.

It was the most essential thing.

In that environment, feeding Marines was not the work I had left behind in the kitchens of Camp Pendleton. It was the same work in its most urgent and most unadorned form. The Overton standard and the 2 a.m. starts and the 2,880 strips of bacon without burning one had all been preparation for this. For the moment when feeding people was not about the standard of the meal but about the fact of it.

Between movements, massive dice games appeared out of nowhere.

Money changed hands that would not matter if the next siren ended differently.

Laughter too loud. Eyes too focused.

The kind of laughter that isn't joy.

It's pressure escaping.

Not the genuine lightness of men who have forgotten where they are or what surrounds them. The particular release of tension that an organism produces when the tension has been held at a level that requires periodic discharge or the system will not hold. Laughter that comes from a place deeper than humor. From the part of a man that needs to release something because release is the only alternative to the kind of accumulation that ends badly.

And then the cigarettes.

Sitting on top of a stockpile of fifty-gallon barrels of jet fuel.

Smoking.

No fear.

Just presence.

The beast had been released on the plane. Fear had been replaced by indifference. I was not being reckless sitting up there. Not performing fearlessness for an audience or making a statement about bravado. I was someone who had already accepted the worst possible outcome and was no longer organizing my behavior around avoiding it.

The jet fuel could ignite.

It didn't change anything.

Because everything had already changed on the plane.

Everything had sharpened.

Colors. Smells. Sound.

The awareness of where my body was in space at all times. The awareness of where the exits were. The awareness of who was near me and what they were capable of.

This was not chaos.

This was order stripped to its most honest form.

The watch had built awareness in the dark. The kitchen had built precision under pressure. The desert sky had offered Orion before I had a name for it. All of it had been preparation for this.

For the particular clarity that arrives when everything unnecessary has been burned away and what remains is the essential self, fully present, fully awake, organized around nothing except what the next moment requires.

Death wasn't dramatic.

It was logistical.

It moved through systems. Through schedules. Through mistakes. Through proximity.

I could feel it passing near me like wind.

Sometimes it touched others.

Sometimes it didn't.

I moved forward anyway.

Because that was what the situation required.

And because the formation was complete.

And because the beast had been released.

And because I had been sentenced to the sand by an institution that had not broken me and I was standing in the smoke and the wrong-smelling air with a rifle in my hand and rounds in the chamber and nothing left to fear because fear had already let go on the plane.

Arrival.

No buildup.

No adjustment.

Just the sand.

And everything it was going to require.

CHAPTER 22

The Alarms

The alarms didn't care what time it was.

That is the first thing to understand about them and everything else follows from it. The alarms were not organized around the human schedule. Not around sleep cycles or meal times or the institutional rhythms that had structured every previous environment I had ever operated inside. Not around day or night, not around the particular human expectation that certain hours carry certain qualities and that the body deserves to know which kind of hour it is currently inside.

The alarms arrived when they arrived.

Not according to any pattern that could be learned and anticipated and prepared for with the particular quality of readiness that preparation allows. Randomly. Or in whatever pattern the incoming threat had been organized by, which was not a pattern accessible to the people on the receiving end of it. The alarm did not announce itself in advance. It simply arrived, at whatever hour it chose, and what happened in the seconds following its arrival was entirely dependent on what the person hearing it had already built inside themselves before it sounded.

Seven seconds.

Maybe ten.

That uncertainty in maybe ten is not imprecision. It is honesty. Because in the moment the alarm sounds the body does not have access to precise measurements. It has access to motion. To the automatic deployment of everything that training has installed deeply enough to operate without conscious instruction. Seven seconds was the margin. Maybe ten. The difference between seven and ten is three seconds. In most contexts, three seconds is nothing. A pause in conversation. A moment of hesitation before a decision. Three seconds of ordinary time that passes without notice.

In a combat zone with missiles incoming, three seconds is everything.

Missiles incoming.

The word incoming carries a specific and irreversible quality in a military context. Outgoing is the round you fire. Outgoing moves away from you. It may do damage elsewhere but it is no longer your immediate problem once it leaves the barrel or the wing or the launcher. Incoming is the opposite. Incoming is moving toward you. Incoming has you as its destination. Incoming is the situation that the entirety of the preparation in every preceding chapter was designed to address and that no amount of preparation actually fully prepares you for until it is real and the alarm is sounding and the margin is seven seconds.

Maybe ten.

You moved or you didn't.

The simplicity of that statement is the fullest possible expression of what the alarm reduced everything to. Not a matrix of options. Not a decision tree with branches. Two outcomes. Two conditions. You moved or you didn't. And everything that determined which of those two conditions you produced was not conscious in the moment of the alarm. It was installed before the alarm. It lived in the body before the alarm sounded and expressed itself through the body the instant it did.

The watch from Chapter 2 had been building this.

Not as a direct preparation for missile alarms. As the installation of a quality of presence that could be sustained at all times and deployed instantly when the instant arrived. The four hours in the dark, the eyes moving near to far, the discipline of attention when nothing was happening so that the attention was available and sharp and already in motion when something was. The watch had been building the body's ability to respond before the mind had fully processed what it was responding to.

Chapter 3 had been building this too.

The sleep that was never fully sleep. The hovering just above unconsciousness. The system that had been reconfigured to treat shutdown as death and had accordingly refused to fully shut down. That adaptation had felt like a cost in the years following the war, a permanent tax on rest that the desert had levied and that no subsequent environment had managed to repeal. But here, in the sand, in the context for which it had been built, it was the difference between seven seconds and no seconds.

You were never fully asleep.

Which meant you were always already in motion when the alarm sounded.

The gas mask.

The chemical threat was the threat that organized everything else around it in a specific way because it was the threat that was invisible until it was too late to do anything about it without the mask already in place. A missile you could see or at least hear in its approach. The impact created a perimeter that was visible and assessable and that you could move away from or shelter from with the particular directional logic of physical threat.

Chemical agents did not work that way.

Chemical agents dispersed. They moved with the air in whatever direction the air was moving, which was not a direction you could predict or defend against directionally. The only defense was the seal between your face and the mask and the integrity of the filter the mask's air passed through. Not distance. Not cover. The mask.

Which is why the mask was always within reach.

Always.

Not within reach in the sense of nearby or accessible with effort. Within reach in the sense that the distance between the sleeping hand and the mask was a distance that could be covered in a fraction of a second, in the dark, without sight, without fully waking, without any conscious process intervening between the alarm and the mask being in place.

The body had memorized the distance.

The body had made the reaching automatic.

So that when the alarm sounded at three in the morning or at noon or in the half-light of a day filtered through smoke from burning oil fields, the body did not need instructions. It had already been given them. Long before the alarm. In the accumulation of every day in that environment when the alarm had not sounded but the body had stayed ready for it anyway.

The alarm didn't care what time it was.

The body didn't either.

That alignment between the arbitrary timing of the alarm and the continuous readiness of the body it was alarming was not accidental. It was the product of exactly the kind of installed discipline that the Corps had been building since the first day of service. Since the watch in the dark. Since the 2 a.m. kitchen. Since the sixteen ovens. Since the parade deck and the plane and the beast released on the final leg of a twenty-two-hour flight toward the sand.

The alarm sounded.

The body moved.

Not after the body assessed the alarm. Not after the conscious mind confirmed that the alarm was the kind of alarm that required the response and not a false alarm or a test or a sound that resembled the alarm but was something else. The body moved first. The mind caught up during the motion. That sequence, body before mind, motion before assessment, is not a failure of deliberation. It is the specific product of a system that has been built to operate at the speed the situation requires.

Seven seconds.

The mask was on.

Maybe ten.

The position was secured.

And then the waiting.

Because after the initial motion the alarm produced came the particular quality of waiting that had no equivalent in any previous experience. The waiting that was not the waiting of Las Pulgas or the waiting of the shrinking list. The waiting of a man in a gas mask in a bunker in the middle of a desert with missiles somewhere in the air above him, not knowing whether the next sound he heard would be the all-clear or something else entirely.

That waiting lasted however long it lasted.

It was never short.

It was never routine.

No matter how many times the alarm sounded. No matter how many times the body deployed itself and the mask went on and the position was taken and the waiting began. Every time was the first time in the specific sense that every time the alarm sounded there was a real possibility that this particular instance would be the one that ended differently.

The all-clear came.

Or it didn't.

When it came, there was no celebration. No release of breath in the theatrical sense. The breath had been controlled throughout. The mask came off. The position was released. The system returned to the readiness that was its permanent state in that environment.

Ready for the next alarm.

Which could come at any time.

Because the alarms didn't care what time it was.

And the body had long since stopped caring either.

That changes you.

Not in ways that announced themselves. Not in ways that were visible from the outside in the moment they were happening. In the deep and quiet way that the most permanent changes happen. In the rewiring that the watch had begun and the kitchen had continued and the desert was completing. The person who returned from each alarm was not the same person who had been sleeping before it sounded. Incrementally. Fractionally. Alarm by alarm. The accumulation of seven-second margins and mask deployments and all-clears that arrived and all-clears that were late and the permanent underlying awareness that the next one might not arrive at all.

That stays.

It stayed long after the desert.

Long after the uniform.

Long after the sand was behind me and the smoke line was no longer the sky and the air no longer smelled wrong.

The body remembered the margin.

Seven seconds.

Maybe ten.

You moved or you didn't.

CHAPTER 23

Always Ready

The gas mask was the pillow.

Not metaphorically. Not as a way of describing the psychological state of someone who could not fully rest because the threat was always present. Literally. The gas mask, the piece of equipment that stood between my face and a chemical agent dispersed through the air of a combat zone, was positioned under my head when I slept.

That placement was not comfort.

It was the most honest possible expression of the environment.

You sleep where you are. You sleep with what you have. You sleep in whatever configuration allows the body the rest it requires while keeping the distance between the sleeping self and the equipment the situation demands at zero. Not nearby. Not within arm's reach. Under the head. The mask reachable without looking for it, without the added seconds of locating it in the dark, without the margin between the alarm sounding and the mask being in place being any wider than the absolute minimum the body could produce.

The boots were within reach.

Same logic. Different category of readiness. The mask addressed the chemical threat. The boots addressed the movement requirement. You cannot move effectively in a combat environment without boots on. Boots within reach meant the time between the alarm and the body being capable of movement was as short as the body could make it. Every second removed from that margin was a second added to the margin that the alarm required.

Seven seconds.

Maybe ten.

Chapter 22 had established what the alarm demanded. Chapter 23 is about what the body had to become in order to meet that demand not once or twice but continuously, through every hour of every day and every night, for the duration of the war.

I didn't sleep fully.

Chapter 3 had described this. The hovering just above sleep. The system that had refused to fully shut down because shutdown in the desert had been indistinguishable from death. The body's adaptation to an environment that offered no safe period of complete unconsciousness and that had accordingly produced a state of permanent partial awareness, present even in the hours of nominal rest, tracking even when the eyes were closed.

What Chapter 3 had described in the context of the return from war, the already-installed hypervigilance I had changed by the desert and did not yet know how permanent the change was, was not the origin of that state.

This was the origin.

This specific environment. These specific conditions. The gas mask pillow and the boots within reach and the alarm that could sound at any hour without warning and the margin of seven seconds that separated someone in a gas mask from someone who had not moved quickly enough.

Here, in this sand, under this smoke-filtered sky, the body had learned the thing that Chapter 3 had described as its permanent inheritance. The body had learned it from necessity. From the daily education of an environment that made full sleep a liability and partial awareness the only survivable option.

You stop going all the way under.

Not as a choice. As an adaptation. The same word Chapter 3 had used for the same process because it was the same process, experienced here in its original context and carried home in its residual form, still running in the body long after the environment that produced it no longer existed.

Everything had sharpened.

Colors.

Smells.

Sound.

This is the specific phenomenology of hypervigilance in a combat environment and it deserves to be understood as something other than fear or paranoia or the psychological symptom it would later be classified as in clinical language. In the environment it was produced by, it was function. Perfect, necessary, adaptive function.

Colors were sharper because color carries information about threat. The particular shade of something moving at the edge of your visual field. The color of smoke and what the color tells you about what is burning and how close it is and in which direction it is moving. The color of the sky at different hours and what the variations in that color communicated about the oil fires and the wind and the atmospheric conditions that determined how chemical agents would move if they were deployed.

Color was data.

Smells carried more information than they had in any previous environment because smell had been established as the first warning system. The wrong smell from Chapter 21. The specific quality of burning that was not ordinary burning. The air carrying things in it that previous air had not carried. The body had recalibrated its relationship with smell the way it had recalibrated its relationship with sleep, assigning it a level of conscious attention that most environments did not require it to receive.

Smell was data.

Sound sorted itself into categories that had not existed before the desert. Not just loud and quiet. Not just near and far. Sound organized itself by what it indicated. The particular quality of incoming versus outgoing that the ear learned to distinguish through the accumulated experience of hearing both enough times to know the difference in their approach. The sound of an alarm that was real versus the sound of equipment that had produced a similar tone. The sound of movement that was human versus the sound of the wind moving through the structures of the camp.

Sound was data.

The awareness of where my body was in space at all times.

That phrase from the source material is one of the most precise descriptions of hypervigilance ever written and it is precisely right. Not the awareness of where other things were in space. The awareness of where my own body was. The continuous proprioceptive monitoring of self-in-space that the environment had installed as a baseline function. Where my feet were. Where my hands were. What my posture communicated and what it was ready to produce. The distance between my body and the nearest cover. The angle between my position and the positions of the people nearest me.

My body was always located.

In every moment.

Without conscious instruction.

The awareness of where exits were.

This one does not require elaboration. It is the most direct possible expression of what the environment had taught and what my body had learned. Every space I occupied, every structure I moved through, every position I took, was assessed immediately and automatically for its exits. Not because I was planning to flee. Because exits were the difference between options and the absence of options and the body had learned, in this environment, that the absence of options was something to be prevented before it arrived rather than addressed after.

The awareness of who was near me and what they were capable of.

This is the social dimension of combat hypervigilance and it is perhaps the most durable of all the adaptations the desert produced. The watch had trained me to read terrain for deviation. WESTPAC had trained me to read people for the same quality. The desert combined both into a continuous ambient assessment of every person within my operational perimeter. Not suspicion. Not paranoia. The functional equivalent of the awareness of exits applied to the human environment. What are the people near me capable of? What are they carrying? What is the quality of their attention and what does that quality indicate about their state and their readiness and their potential as either asset or threat?

This was not chaos.

This was order stripped to its most honest form.

That phrase deserves to sit and be understood. Because the external environment was genuinely chaotic. The smoke and the alarms and the wrong-smelling air and the live rounds and the unapproved medication and the oil fields burning and the missiles incoming. The external environment was everything that the word chaos is meant to describe.

But inside me, built by the watch and the kitchen and the standard and the WESTPAC and the plane and the beast released, there was no chaos.

There was the most fundamental order available.

The order of a system operating exactly as it was designed to operate, in the environment it was designed to operate in, without the friction of doubt or the interference of unresolved fear because the fear had let go on the plane and what remained was clarity.

Death wasn't dramatic.

It was logistical.

It moved through systems. Through schedules. Through mistakes. Through proximity.

You could feel it passing near you like wind.

Sometimes it touched others.

Sometimes it didn't.

We danced with it anyway.

Not because death was welcome. Not because the indifference that had replaced fear on the plane was the same as carelessness or the reckless disregard for self-preservation that inexperience sometimes produces. The indifference was the acceptance of the full range of possible outcomes. Including the one that ends everything. Including the one that passes close enough to feel but does not land. Including everything in between.

You accept the full range.

And then you move.

Because movement is what the situation requires and the situation is what it is and the body has been built to meet exactly this situation with exactly the quality of readiness that the gas mask pillow and the boots within reach and the sharpened colors and the sorted sounds and the always-located body represent.

Always ready.

Not as a slogan. Not as the aspirational language of a recruitment poster. As a physical state. A condition of the body. The actual literal truth of a man in a combat zone who has been built, chapter by chapter, to be exactly what this moment requires.

Always ready.

That changes you.

Not sometimes. Not if the deployment is long enough or intense enough or if the right conditions are present. Always. The change is the adaptation. The adaptation is the learning. The learning is what the body does when it has no choice but to become equal to what is being demanded of it.

The gas mask pillow.

The boots within reach.

The sharpened world.

The located body.

The exits always known.

The people always assessed.

The death moving through the air like wind.

Always ready.

That changes you.

And it does not change back.

CHAPTER 24

Food Runs

The mission was not glamorous.

No mission in support of combat operations is glamorous when you are inside it rather than describing it from a distance. But the food runs had a specific quality of unglamour that went beyond the ordinary absence of drama in logistical work. They required driving through what had recently been the most dangerous places on earth to deliver something that people were going to consume and then forget about. They required navigating landscape that had been organized, until very recently, around the systematic effort to kill anyone moving through it in the direction we were moving.

The landscape had changed.

The danger had not entirely gone with it.

We drove through what used to be front lines.

The past tense in that sentence is doing important work.

Used to be. Not former front lines in the sense of a location that had been designated as a boundary at some point in the past and had long since been reclassified into something else. Used to be in the most immediate sense. In the sense of something that had been one thing very recently and had become another thing not because the threat had been resolved but because the advance had moved forward and the front line had moved with it and what was left behind was the evidence of where it had been.

Burnt vehicles.

The vehicles were a specific kind of evidence. Not destroyed in the abstract. Burnt. The word carries its own weight. A vehicle that has been burnt is not simply a vehicle that no longer functions. It is a vehicle that has been subjected to a particular kind of force that leaves a particular kind of mark. The metal warped and blackened. The interior gone. The shape recognizable as what it had been while being completely transformed from what it was.

You drove past them and you did not stop to look.

Not because they were not worth looking at. Because stopping to look was not what the mission allowed and was not what the road required and was not what the Marines at the other end of the route were waiting for. You registered them the way the always-ready awareness of Chapter 23 registered everything. Continuously. Without full conscious processing. Adding them to the accumulated inventory of what the war had left on the ground.

Bodies.

That word stands alone in the source material and it stands alone here because it deserves to.

Bodies is the plain word for the most consequential thing a human being can encounter in a landscape. Not casualties. Not the fallen. Not the language that distance produces to make the fact of death less immediate. Bodies. The physical reality of people who had been alive and were no longer alive and had not yet been removed from the places where that transition had occurred.

You drove past them.

You registered them the same way you registered the burnt vehicles. Continuously. Without full conscious processing. Adding them to the inventory.

But bodies are not the same as vehicles.

The body knows this even when the operational requirement is to treat them as equivalent, to maintain the pace and the focus and the forward momentum that the mission requires. Something in the system receives the information of a body differently than it receives the information of a burnt vehicle, registers it at a depth that is below the operational layer, stores it in the place that Chapter 4 described as the body's own account. The account that runs whether you are paying attention to it or not.

We weren't there to fight.

We were there to feed.

Those two sentences are the full statement of the chapter's meaning and they need to be held together to understand what they contain. Not we weren't there to fight and feeding was the consolation prize. Not we weren't there to fight as a diminishment of the mission. As a distinction. As the specific and precise truth of what the food runs were in the context of everything surrounding them.

The war was organized around fighting. Around the application of force in the direction of objectives defined by people who had access to the operational picture in its entirety. The Howitzer unit twenty clicks behind the front lines was part of that application, feeling the response even without seeing the impact, always moving forward into the same danger from a different distance.

The food runs were organized around something else.

Around the recognition that the people applying the force were human beings whose bodies required fuel to continue applying it. Around the understanding that fighting without eating is not sustainable beyond a certain point and that the point is reached faster than anyone who has not been in that situation imagines. Around the particular truth that I had been building toward since Cook School at Parris Island: that feeding people is not a lesser mission than the missions it supports.

It is the mission that makes all other missions possible.

Two hot meals a day if everything went right.

One MRE.

Sometimes less.

The specificity of that accounting is important. Two hot meals a day if everything went right. If everything went right. Which means there were days when everything did not go right. When the route was compromised or the timing was off or the operational picture had shifted in ways that made the food run impossible or inadvisable or later than the Marines at the other end of it needed it to be.

On those days: one MRE.

Sometimes less.

An MRE is Meals Ready to Eat. Self-contained. No preparation required. Designed for exactly the situations where preparation is not possible. Functional fuel that addresses the body's requirement without addressing anything else that food can address when conditions allow it to. No warmth. No gathering. No circle. No plate shared without hesitation.

Just fuel.

The food runs existed to prevent the one MRE days from becoming every day. To ensure that the hot meals arrived as often as the mission allowed. To put something in the hands of the Marines at the forward positions that was warmer and more real and more human than the self-contained alternative.

Food runs to the front lines mattered as much as ammunition.

That equivalence is not rhetorical exaggeration.

It is operational fact.

A Marine who has not eaten cannot hold a position. Cannot maintain the alertness that the alarm system requires. Cannot sustain the seven-second response time that the margin demands. Cannot make the decisions at the speed the situation requires. Cannot be what the mission needs me to be. The food that arrived on those runs was not the food of the courtyard or the food of my mother's Thanksgiving table or the food that the circle in the Philippines had shared without hesitation.

It was ammunition of a different kind.

Hot food meant morale.

Hot food meant something still functioned.

In an environment where so much had been stripped to its most essential form, where the smoke had replaced the sky and the gas mask had replaced the pillow and the dice games were pressure escaping rather than joy, the arrival of hot food was the signal that the system was still working. That somewhere behind the forward positions there were people whose job was to make sure the Marines eating were fed and who were doing that job regardless of the terrain I had to cross to do it.

That mattered.

Not abstractly.

Specifically.

To specific men sitting on whatever would hold them in positions that were no longer camps, eating fast and quiet and standing or sitting on the ground, with the awareness of exits and the sharpened senses and the always-located body, taking in something hot.

We delivered meals forward, into places that didn't resemble camps anymore.

Men ate fast.

Quiet.

Standing.

Sitting on anything that would hold them.

That image is the full expression of what the courtyard had shown in its opposite. The courtyard had been the circle. The sharing without hesitation. The everyone eats or no one eats. The communal recognition that food is not just fuel but the physical expression of a community's relationship with itself.

This was not the courtyard.

This was men in a combat zone eating as fast as the situation allowed because the situation did not offer the courtyard and we knew it and we ate anyway because the body required it and the body requiring something was sufficient reason to meet the requirement.

And I was the one who had driven through burnt vehicles and bodies to put something in their hands that was hot.

Not because it was glamorous.

Because it was the mission.

Because feeding Marines had been the mission since Cook School at Parris Island and it remained the mission in the sand and the mission did not change because the route to executing it had become more dangerous.

The standard Overton had given was still present.

Not in the form of the best mess hall on Camp Pendleton. In the form of someone who drove to the front lines to make sure the Marines there had something to eat because that was what the standard required and the standard did not negotiate with the difficulty of the path to meeting it.

We weren't there to fight.

We were there to feed.

And that mattered.

Not because anyone acknowledged it.

Not because the food runs appeared in any operational report as anything other than logistical support.

Because the men sitting on the ground eating fast and quiet were sitting there alive. And alive meant the mission continued. And the mission continuing meant the war moved forward. And the war moving forward meant the front line advanced and the line that twenty clicks behind became thirty and eventually the line reached the place where the ceasefire was declared and the sand was left behind.

Because food runs, conducted through terrain that no longer resembled anything other than what a war leaves behind, had been part of what made that possible.

That was enough.

That had always been enough.

A Marine cook who had driven through destruction not to fight but to feed understood something about the nature of service that the purely operational version of service did not fully contain.

That you do not have to carry a weapon to sustain the people who do.

That the mission is not only what happens at the front.

That the standard applies in every direction.

Even into the places that used to be front lines.

Even past the burnt vehicles.

Even past the bodies.

Especially then.

CHAPTER 25

What Was Left Behind

The advance moved forward.

That is how war works at the operational level. The line moves. Territory is gained. The positions that defined the front yesterday are behind the front today. The mission continues in the direction it has been moving and the people executing the mission move with it, forward, always forward, toward the next objective, the next position, the next boundary that needs to be crossed.

What stays behind is everything the advance left.

We moved through what had already been fought over.

That phrase is precise in a way that requires attention. Not through what had been cleared. Not through what had been secured or pacified or resolved in the language that military operations use when they want to describe the completion of a thing. Through what had already been fought over. The fight was over. The fighting had moved forward with the advance. What remained was the aftermath. The physical record of what had happened when two forces occupied the same space and one of them had not survived the occupation.

Burnt vehicles.

They appeared again here the way they had appeared on the food runs, registered by the always-ready awareness without full conscious processing, accumulated in the body's account. But on the food runs they had been peripheral. Adjacent to the route. Present in the landscape that was being passed through. Here they were the landscape. The advance had moved through exactly this ground. The burnt vehicles were not beside the story. They were the story. They were what the story had produced and left behind when it moved forward.

Each one had been a vehicle before it was a burnt vehicle.

That observation is not obvious and it is not rhetorical.

A vehicle carries things. People. Equipment. The logistical requirements of an operation. It moves. It provides mobility to people and things that would otherwise be stationary. It is functional, purposeful, organized around the service it provides to the people using it. And then something happens to it and it is no longer any of those things. It is a burnt vehicle. Warped. Blackened. Still recognizable as the shape of what it had been. No longer capable of being what it had been. Standing in the landscape as the most permanent possible record of what had occurred here.

The burnt vehicles didn't lie.

Twisted metal.

That phrase does the same work as burnt vehicles but from a different angle. Twisted suggests force applied beyond the design tolerance of the thing it twisted. It suggests the meeting of something that was built to hold a shape and something powerful enough to change that shape against the resistance of its construction. Twisted metal is the evidence of the moment when force exceeded structure. When what had been built to resist gave way.

The war had twisted things that had been built not to twist.

Silence.

That is the third element and it is the one that stays longest because it is the one that has no physical form to fade or corrode or eventually be cleared. Silence is the absence of the sounds that the fight produced. The absence of the voices and the engines and the weapons and the alarms and the particular audio signature of a combat environment in full operation. All of that was gone because the people who had generated it were gone, forward with the advance or not forward at all.

What remained was the silence of a place where something large had happened and had ended.

That silence is not the silence of Chapter 2.

Chapter 2's silence was the intentional watchful silence of a man standing his post in the desert darkness, actively present, filling the quiet with the quality of my attention. That silence was inhabited. Purposeful. Generated by the discipline of someone who understood that stillness was not emptiness but a form of full engagement.

The silence of the fought-over ground was different.

It was the silence of absence. Of a place that had been full and was now empty. That had contained living systems and no longer contained them. That had been the location of the most concentrated human activity imaginable and now contained only its residue.

It wasn't cleaned up.

That fact carries more weight than it might initially appear to carry. In most environments, the aftermath of a destructive event is eventually cleaned up. The evidence is removed. The landscape is restored to something that resembles what it was before. This is partly practical, partly psychological. Practical because the evidence is a hazard or an obstacle or a liability. Psychological because human beings have a relationship with the visible record of catastrophe that makes its continued presence difficult to sustain indefinitely.

Here it wasn't cleaned up because the advance had not paused to clean it up.

The advance moved forward.

Everything else stayed.

It wasn't reset.

That word reset is important because it carries the institutional implication that there is a baseline state that can be restored after the deviation has ended. That what is there now is a departure from a norm and that the norm can be returned to. Reset implies reversibility. Implies that the state before the thing happened can be recovered if the right steps are taken in the right order.

The ground that had been fought over could not be reset.

Not because the physical evidence could not eventually be removed. Because the fought-over quality of the ground was permanent regardless of what happened to the physical evidence. The ground knew what had happened on it in the way that places know the things that have occurred in them, not through language or memory or the conscious record that human beings maintain, but through the particular quality of presence that locations carry after they have been the site of something that changes everything that comes after.

It was still there.

All of it.

The burnt vehicles and the twisted metal and the silence and the fought-over quality of the ground and the particular kind of light that filtered through the smoke above it all. Still there. Unchanged by the fact that the people who had been there had moved forward. Still holding everything it had witnessed. Still present in the full, unresolved, unacknowledged way of things that have not been addressed.

And once you saw it, you carried it.

That closing line of the original source needs to be the closing of this chapter because it is the most important line in the chapter and possibly one of the most important lines in the book.

Not because of what it says about the ground.

Because of what it says about the person who moved through it.

The ground could not carry what had happened on it in a human sense. It did not have the system that carries things. It did not have the body's account that Chapter 4 had described, running whether you were paying attention to it or not, adding to the tab without ceremony or acknowledgment.

But I did.

And the moment I moved through the ground that had already been fought over, the moment my eyes registered the burnt vehicles and the twisted metal and the silence, the moment my always-ready awareness cataloged what it was seeing and added it to the inventory, the carrying began.

Not as a choice.

As a consequence.

You cannot see what I saw in that landscape and not carry it. Not because it is too heavy to set down, though it is. Not because the mind refuses to release it, though the mind does refuse. Because the seeing is the carrying. Because the moment the information enters the body it becomes part of the body's account and the account does not offer the option of removal.

Chapter 4 had described the body as loyal.

Loyal to the environment that shaped it. Loyal to the threat it was trained to prepare for. Loyal to the version of the world it learned to survive in.

The body was loyal to this too.

To what it had seen.

To the burnt vehicles and the twisted metal and the silence of a place where something had happened that the advance had moved past without pausing to name.

The advance moved forward.

The body carried what the advance left.

Not by choice.

Because it had been there.

Because it had seen.

Because seeing is the beginning of carrying and carrying does not have a natural end point.

The war was not only what you did in it.

It was what you witnessed.

What you moved through.

What the advance left behind and what your body picked up as it moved through that leaving.

And once you saw it, you carried it.

Without asking.

Without choosing.

For as long as the body held.

CHAPTER 26

The Work No One Talks About

War is not only what it looks like from the outside.

From the outside it looks like the things that appear in the reports and the briefings and the operational accounts that get written when the shooting has stopped and the people with the authority to write those accounts sit down to describe what happened. It looks like the advance and the objectives and the positions taken and the positions held and the particular geometry of force applied to ground over time. It looks like the things that get named and acknowledged and entered into the record as the content of what the war was.

From the inside it looks like everything else.

The outside version and the inside version share the same timeline and the same geography and some of the same events. But they are not the same account. The outside version is organized around the things that mattered operationally. The inside version is organized around the things that had to happen so that the operational things could happen. Around the support. The maintenance. The unglamorous continuous work of keeping a combat operation functional in the gaps between the moments that get named.

That work does not appear in the reports.

Nobody talks about it.

Nobody, after the fact, says let me tell you about the logistics. Let me tell you about the supply chain. Let me tell you about the particular category of work that existed in the space between the missions. The work that had no heroism attached to it and no narrative arc and no moment of resolution where a thing was accomplished that could be pointed to as evidence of something meaningful.

They put me on shit watch.

There it is.

In the middle of a war in the desert, with the smoke line above and the live rounds chambered and the gas mask always within reach and the alarms that arrived without schedule and the food runs through burnt vehicles and bodies, I was assigned to shit watch.

Shit watch is exactly what it sounds like.

Human waste.

A combat zone generates it. The people inside a combat zone generate it. The bodies of the Marines eating two hot meals a day when everything went right and one MRE when it didn't and sometimes less than that are human bodies and human bodies produce waste regardless of the operational picture. The war did not pause for this. The bodies of twenty-five thousand Marines at the height of the base camp's population did not hold what they produced until the operational picture was more convenient.

The waste had to go somewhere.

And the waste going somewhere required a system. A method. A person assigned to implement the method consistently so that the waste that the operational Marines produced did not become a sanitation crisis in the middle of an active combat theater.

That person was me.

Jet fuel.

A stick.

No mask.

No protection.

The method was not complicated. The fifty-gallon drums that had appeared in Chapter 23 as the barrels a man with no fear sat on top of while smoking cigarettes served a secondary purpose. The waste was collected. The jet fuel was added. The stick was used to combine them. The combination was burned.

That is the full description.

There is no version of that task that is anything other than what it is. No framing that elevates it. No language that removes the specific quality of what was being done and replaced it with something more palatable. No mask between the face of the person doing it and the air the task produced.

Just doing what had to be done.

That phrase is the complete statement of my relationship with shit watch and it is the right phrase not because it minimizes the task but because it is precisely true. The task had to be done. It was assigned to him. He did it. The gap between those three facts is where character lives.

Not the character of someone who embraced the assignment or found meaning in it in the traditional sense of meaning. The character of someone who had been built, across every chapter of this book, on the principle that the standard applies everywhere. That the work deserves to be done correctly regardless of whether it is the kind of work that gets recognized or acknowledged or entered into any record that anyone will ever read.

Shit watch was not going to appear in any record.

It was going to be done anyway.

At the full standard of what done correctly meant.

Because that is what the standard requires. Not only in the kitchen that dignitaries come to eat at. Not only in the mess hall that wins the designation of best on Camp Pendleton. In every task the situation assigns. Including the ones with no audience and no acknowledgment and no language available to describe them without making people uncomfortable.

Especially those.

Because the discipline that only appears when it is visible is not discipline. It is performance. Discipline is what you bring when no one is watching and the task is unglamorous and the air around it makes your eyes water and there is no mask between your face and what the task produces.

War isn't just fighting.

It's everything in between.

That closing from the original source is the thesis of the chapter and it deserves to be understood as something larger than a commentary on shit watch. It is a description of what war actually is from the inside of it.

Fighting is the part that gets described. The part that appears in the accounts and the reports and the stories that get told at bars and reunions and in the books that are written about conflicts. Fighting is what war looks like from the outside.

Everything in between is what war is from the inside.

The filling of sandbags before the position is taken. The maintenance of equipment between the operations that require it. The food runs through terrain that used to be front lines. The shit watch conducted in the space between the alarms. The particular daily continuity of a combat operation that keeps the fighting possible and that consists almost entirely of work that will never be named in any account of what happened.

The Marine Corps understood this.

Not in the language of heroism or narrative. In the language of assignment. In the understanding that the operation required everything that it required and that everything it required would be assigned to someone and that the person assigned to it would do it because doing it was what the operation needed and the operation was what they were there for.

I did it.

Not reluctantly. Not with the particular performance of suffering that unglamorous work sometimes produces in people who want their willingness to do it acknowledged as a sacrifice. Without drama. Without complaint. With the same quality of attention that the 2 a.m. kitchen had required and that the sixteen ovens had required and that the food runs had required.

Jet fuel. A stick. No mask. No protection.

The task assigned.

The task done.

At the standard.

In the space between the things that get talked about.

In the full understanding that this is also what service means. Not only the moments that get named. Also the ones that don't. Also the ones that no one talks about because there is no language available for them that preserves the dignity of the person who did them.

But dignity does not require language.

It requires the person who does the task to bring to it the same quality of presence they bring to every other task. To treat the work as worthy of the standard not because the work earns that designation but because the standard does not have exceptions.

Shit watch.

Jet fuel. A stick. No mask. No protection.

War isn't just fighting.

It's everything in between.

And everything in between deserves to be done right.

CHAPTER 27

The Lesson

A Staff Sergeant left his weapon behind.

That sentence needs to be understood in its full context before anything else is said about what followed it. Not left his weapon behind in the sense of setting it down somewhere temporarily and walking away without it. Left his weapon behind in a combat zone. In an environment where the weapon was not equipment in the ordinary sense of the word, not a tool you carried when the task required it and set aside when it didn't. Where the weapon was the margin. The seven seconds. The difference between the situation having options and the situation having none.

In a combat zone, you do not leave your weapon.

That is not an aspiration or a guideline or a principle that reasonable people might weigh against competing considerations and arrive at different conclusions about. It is a rule. An absolute one. One of the rules whose absolute quality is not bureaucratic but existential. The weapon is the margin between the person who has options and the person who does not. Leaving it is not a procedural error. It is the removal of your own margin in the most literal possible sense.

That doesn't happen.

Except that it did.

A Staff Sergeant, a man who had earned the rank, who had been through the training, who understood exactly what the rule was and exactly why it existed with the absoluteness it possessed, had left his weapon in a combat zone.

For days he unraveled.

The unraveling is worth describing because it is not what the word unraveled is usually used to mean. It was not dramatic collapse. Not the visible, public disintegration of a man who has lost the capacity to maintain the appearance of function. That kind of unraveling can be identified and addressed and contained by the institutional systems that exist precisely for that purpose.

This was quieter.

The unraveling of a man who knew exactly what he had done and exactly what it meant and exactly what the institutional response to what he had done would be if the wrong person knew it had happened. The unraveling of someone who was carrying a piece of information that was too heavy to carry alone and too dangerous to share and that was therefore being carried in silence, in the particular private weight of a thing that cannot be set down and cannot be spoken and cannot be resolved by any action the person carrying it has the authority to take.

He could not undo it.

He could not report it without consequence that would reach beyond the incident itself into the full arc of everything he had built and everything he had left behind and everyone who was depending on what he came back as.

He could not find the weapon alone because finding it required acknowledging it was missing and acknowledging it was missing required the reporting he was trying to avoid.

So he unraveled.

Day by day. In the particular quiet way of a man who is managing something that the management of is costing him more than the thing itself.

Then the message came.

Not through official channels. Not as the first step in the formal process that the institutional response to a lost weapon in a combat zone would have initiated. As a message. Passed in the way that some of the most important communications in any institution pass, not through the architecture of official process but through the human network that operates alongside it. Person to person. At the level of the situation itself rather than at the level of the documentation of the situation.

I don't need to know who has it.

Just have it back by morning.

Sit with those two sentences.

The first sentence is the most significant. Not because of what it says but because of what it doesn't say. It doesn't say bring it to me. It doesn't say tell me what happened. It doesn't say give me the name of the person responsible so that the institutional response can be organized around that name. It says I don't need to know who has it. It says the information about who is not the information that matters.

What matters is the second sentence.

Just have it back by morning.

The weapon back. By morning. That is the resolution the situation requires. Not a confession. Not a reckoning. Not the full deployment of the institutional accountability apparatus that a lost weapon in a combat zone would ordinarily activate. The weapon back by morning. The margin restored. The operational reality returned to what it needed to be.

The method of that restoration was not the commanding officer's concern.

And it was.

No paperwork.

That two-word line deserves its own full development because it is doing more work than it appears to be doing. No paperwork means no official record. No official record means the incident does not enter the institutional memory in the form that would follow the Staff Sergeant forward through every subsequent moment of his service. No paperwork means the person who had unraveled for days carrying something he could not set down and could not speak was being given the opportunity to set it down without the weight of permanent documentation added to the weight of the thing itself.

No paperwork was not permissiveness.

It was precision.

The commanding officer had assessed the situation with the specific clarity of someone who understood what the operational requirement was and what the human requirement was and that in this instance both requirements pointed in the same direction. The weapon needed to come back. The Staff Sergeant needed to still be functional. The unit needed to move forward without the particular kind of damage that a formal accountability process would have produced in the person being held formally accountable.

And it was.

By morning, the weapon was back.

The Staff Sergeant was back.

Not the same as before the incident, because no one is the same after the thing that makes them unravel for days even when the resolution comes without formal consequence. But functional. Present. Capable of being what the situation needed him to be.

Lesson delivered.

I was watching all of this.

Not from a position of authority. Not as the person with the responsibility to resolve the situation or the information to understand all of its dimensions. As someone present in the environment where it occurred, with the particular quality of attention that the watch had built and the kitchen had refined and that everything preceding this chapter had been developing into the capacity to read human situations the way I had learned to read terrain.

He saw the unraveling.

He heard the message.

He understood, without requiring an explanation, what had happened and what the resolution meant.

And I received the lesson that the resolution delivered.

Not the lesson about weapons and the rules governing them. That lesson was not new. He had known that rule and its rationale from the first day of service.

The lesson about leadership.

About the difference between accountability and punishment. About the distinction between holding someone to the standard and destroying someone with the standard. About the understanding that the institutional response to a failure is not always the right response, that the right response depends on what the situation actually requires rather than on what the institution's procedure for this category of situation specifies.

The commanding officer had not ignored the rule.

He had served the rule's actual purpose.

The rule existed to ensure that weapons were present and functional in the hands of people who needed them. The rule's purpose was operational readiness. The commanding officer's response had restored operational readiness without destroying the person whose lapse had temporarily compromised it.

That was not a lesser version of accountability.

It was a higher one.

I had experienced accountability from both ends of the spectrum in the chapters preceding this one. Chapter 12 had been the Sergeants making me do pushups while mentoring me simultaneously, accountability delivered with full force and full care, the consequence present and the person still intact at the end of it. Chapter 19 had been the institution reducing me to the last name on a list and removing me from the unit I had built myself inside without explanation, accountability deployed as targeting rather than as development.

Chapter 27 was the third form.

Accountability as the quiet resolution of a human failure in a way that restored the operational requirement without sacrificing the person who had failed to meet it. Not loudly. Not with the institutional apparatus of formal process. With a message that offered the outcome the situation needed and asked for nothing in return except that the outcome be delivered.

I don't need to know who has it.

Just have it back by morning.

That is leadership at the level that matters most.

Not the level of strategy or command or the management of large operational forces. The level of the individual human being and what that individual needs in order to continue to function with dignity in conditions that have already asked more of them than dignity usually survives.

The weapon came back.

No paperwork.

Lesson delivered.

Not the lesson the institution would have specified for this situation.

The right one.

The one that a young Marine from St. Louis who had been building a library of leadership examples across every chapter of this book would carry forward into every kitchen and every team and every moment of difficult human management that waited on the other side of the desert.

The lesson that the standard is not a weapon to be used against the people it governs.

It is the structure that holds them.

And holding them sometimes means knowing what not to know.

And trusting the morning to bring back what it needs to bring.

CHAPTER 28

Orion

At night, I looked up again.

Not for the first time.

That is the most important thing to understand about this moment before anything else is said about it. Not for the first time. The looking up had been happening long before the desert. Long before the sand and the smoke line and the missiles incoming and the seven-second margin and the gas mask pillow and everything that Part V had been accumulating in the body's account.

The looking up had been happening on the Pacific.

Chapter 13 had described it. Standing on the deck of the LST in the middle of the ocean at night, the ship moving through the dark Pacific on its own schedule, the stars present in the way that things are present before you have language for them, before meaning has been assigned. Looking up at a sky so vast and so untouched by city light that the universe felt close in a way it never felt on land. Looking without knowing what I was looking at. Without the name. Without the framework.

The ocean planted something the desert would later name.

That line from Chapter 13 was not rhetorical.

It was exact.

This is the naming.

The desert does not whisper.

It does not ask permission. It strips everything down to truth. At night, when the heat finally loosens its grip and the sky opens fully, the stars do not decorate the darkness. They dominate it. Out there, under a sky untouched by city light, the universe feels close enough to touch. You stop being impressed by noise. You stop pretending. You start listening.

I had been listening for a long time.

Before I knew what I was listening for.

On the Pacific, the nights had offered a sky that was the same sky but a different experience of it. The Pacific sky was present but still connected to the world below. Still reachable by the sounds and the lights and the motion of the ship moving through it. Still part of a journey that had a destination and a timeline and the institutional rhythms of a deployment in progress.

The desert sky was different.

Saudi Arabia. Iraq. Kuwait.

The desert had stripped everything away. The heat had pressed down during the day with the particular indifference that Part I had described, bending the air above the sand into waves, distorting distance, burning away everything that was not essential. Rank. Comfort. The particular pretenses that any organized human environment generates simply by being organized. The desert did not maintain pretense. It removed it.

What was left when the pretense was gone was what was actually there.

And at night, when the heat released its grip, what was actually there was the sky.

I lay in the sand.

Not deliberately. Not as a chosen act of contemplation. Someone who had been awake and operational for hours finding a horizontal surface that was available, in an environment that offered horizontal surfaces only in the form of the sand itself, because the body required some approximation of rest even if rest was not fully available.

The gas mask was nearby.

The boots were within reach.

The body was never fully down.

But the eyes were open and the sky was above and the accumulated weight of what Part V had placed in the body's account was present in its full unresolved totality. The burnt vehicles and the twisted metal and the silence of the fought-over ground. The bodies registered without processing. The alarms and the seven-second margins. The shit watch and the dice games and the laughter that was pressure escaping rather than joy. The food runs through destruction. The Staff Sergeant's weapon and the lesson about what leadership at its highest form actually requires.

All of it present.

All of it carried.

The sky opened.

And there it was.

A pattern.

Not scattered like everything else above it. Not random. Structured.

Three stars. Perfectly aligned. Cutting clean across the darkness like something had been placed there deliberately, with intention, with precision. While the rest of the sky spread out in all directions, vast and complicated and beyond any single mind to hold, these three held still. They didn't drift. They didn't blur. They simply were.

Orion.

Not seen for the first time. Recognized for the first time. The distinction between those two experiences is total and it is the most important thing that happens in this chapter.

On the Pacific I had looked at this same pattern and had known that something was there without knowing what it was. Had registered the three stars in formation without having the name to attach to them, without the framework to understand what he was looking at, without the particular significance that a name makes possible once it arrives.

He had been looking at Orion for months without knowing it.

And now I knew.

The name arrived the way names arrive when the thing they describe has been present long enough for the naming to feel like recognition rather than introduction. Not a new piece of information being received. An existing reality being confirmed. The thing had been there before the name. The name was simply the moment the relationship became conscious.

Orion.

The word settled into the body the way the deepest things settle. Not loudly. Not with ceremony. With the quiet authority of something that is true and has always been true and is only now being understood as true by the person who has been living inside its truth without the language to describe it.

And with the name came the recognition of what the name carried.

The Maker.

Chapter 1 had described it. In that stripped-down state, looking up at a sky I had no framework to understand, something shifted. He wasn't searching for God. He wasn't in a place of prayer or ritual. He was a young Marine lying in the sand in the middle of a war zone, running on insufficient sleep, trained for violence, surrounded by uncertainty on every side.

But Orion was there.

And in the desert, in that original encounter, the recognition had arrived that the order I was seeing was not accidental. That the structure above me was not random. That there was a mind behind what I was looking at, a presence behind the pattern, something that had built this and was still, in some way I had no words for yet, attending to it.

To me.

In the sand. In the war. In the dark.

That encounter had happened before this chapter.

This chapter was when it completed itself.

Because on the Pacific I had looked at the pattern without the name and the name had not yet carried the weight it was about to carry. But now, lying in the sand of the desert after everything Part V had accumulated, after the burnt vehicles and the bodies and the alarms and the shit watch and the food runs and the quiet lesson of a commanding officer who knew what not to know, now the name arrived in a context that made its full meaning available.

Orion.

Not a constellation memorized from a book. Not mythology encountered in a classroom. A constant. A fixed point above every desert and every ocean and every kitchen and every parade deck and every difficult thing a man is asked to carry through the world.

In a place where nothing else was certain, it remained.

Everything else in the sand was uncertain. The operational picturc changed. The front line moved. The assignments changed. The week's plan dissolved into the hour's requirement. The alarms arrived without schedule. Death moved through the air like wind and touched who it touched without pattern or warning or the particular fairness that human beings want from a universe that does not organize itself around what human beings want.

Nothing was certain.

But when I looked up, Orion was there.

Exactly where it had been the night before.

Exactly where it would be the night after.

Rising. Setting. Reappearing regardless of what had happened during the day. Regardless of what had been seen or done or survived. The belt cutting clean across the darkness again with the message that had always been the same:

Structure exists beyond the chaos on the ground.

Order doesn't have to be invented. It already is.

You just have to be stripped down enough to see it.

The desert had stripped me down.

Everything before this moment had been the stripping. The watch and the kitchen and the standard and the parade deck and the plane and the beast released and the sand and the smoke and the alarms and the bodies and the shit watch and all of it, all of the accumulated weight of the formation, had been the stripping away of everything that was not essential until what remained was a man lying in the sand looking up at three stars in formation and understanding for the first time what I had been looking at for months.

Reliance. Not belief.

Belief can be shaken.

Reliance keeps you steady.

He had not been believing in Orion. He had been relying on it before I had language for the reliance. The Pacific had taught me to look up before I knew what I was looking for. The desert had given me what I was looking for before I knew what it meant. And now, in this moment, with the name arrived and the recognition complete and the full accumulated weight of the formation behind him, the meaning assembled itself.

The Maker behind the pattern.

The same hand that set those three stars in formation, steady and unmistakable above every desert and ocean and battlefield on earth, was the same hand that had placed me here. In this sand. Under this sky. At this exact moment in a life that had been building toward this recognition since the first night on the Pacific when a young Marine looked up at a vast dark ocean sky and felt something I did not yet have words for.

He had the words now.

Or the beginning of them.

The words would take years to fully develop. The relationship between me and Orion was not complete in this moment in the desert. It was recognized. Named. Claimed as the thing it had been becoming since the ocean. And from this recognition it would grow into something that would outlast the war by decades.

Every company I would build would carry the name.

Every new mission accepted. Every venture committed to. Every kitchen and every team and every table and every moment of difficult human leadership and every return to the beginning that a life of service requires of the people serious enough to live it.

Orion.

The name of every company. The cornerstone. The anchor.

He didn't know all of that yet.

He knew only what the desert was showing him.

Same sky. Same pattern. The thing that had been there before I had language for it now carrying the language and everything the language unlocked.

In a place where nothing else was certain, it remained.

That mattered.

Not in the sentimental sense. Not in the way that comfort matters when comfort is what is needed.

In the deepest possible sense.

The sense in which something that remains while everything else shifts is not just reassurance but evidence. Evidence that beneath the operational chaos and the smoke line and the missiles incoming and the bodies on the food run roads and the accumulated weight of everything Part V had placed in the body's account, there was a structure that the chaos could not reach. An order that existed independently of whether the people living inside the chaos could see it or access it or find language for it.

Orion was the visible expression of that structure.

Three stars in formation. Always in formation. Unmoved by what happened below them. Present above every desert and ocean and kitchen and difficult human moment that has ever required a person to look up and find that something is still there.

He looked up.

It was there.

The circle that had begun on the Pacific, with a young Marine looking at a sky I could not name, closed here.

In the sand.

After the war.

In the moment that everything the formation had been building toward finally arrived at the thing it had been building toward all along.

Not toughness.

Not fearlessness.

Something quieter.

An internal alignment between pressure and purpose. Between knowing when to move and knowing when to hold. Between the discipline the Corps had installed and something older and quieter underneath it that Orion spoke to directly.

The sand taught me how to endure.

The stars taught me how to orient.

And Orion taught me, without a single word, that there was a Maker behind the order I was seeing. That I was not navigating alone. That the same hand that set those three stars in formation was the same hand that had placed me here.

I held onto that.

The way you hold onto the only thing that doesn't move.

In a place where nothing else was certain.

It remained.

That was enough.

It had always been enough.

Seek him that maketh the seven stars and Orion, and turneth the shadow of death into the morning, and maketh the day dark with night: that calleth for the waters of the sea, and poureth them out upon the face of the earth: The Lord is his name.

Amos 5:8

I didn't find Orion.

Orion found me.

In the darkness. In the stripping away of everything that was not essential. In the sand and the smoke and the weight of everything the war had placed in the body's account without asking permission and without offering receipt.

It found me when I had nothing left to hold onto except what was fixed above the chaos.

And it did not guide me out of the darkness.

It guided me through it.

There is a difference.

Out of the darkness means the darkness ends. Means you arrive somewhere the darkness has not reached. Means the hard thing is behind you and what is ahead is something other than hard.

Through the darkness means the darkness is real and you move through it anyway. With the fixed point above you. With the three stars in formation cutting clean across the sky regardless of what is happening on the ground below them. With the knowledge that the Maker who set those stars in their place set you in yours. At this moment. In this sand. For this particular passage through the dark.

Orion lit up my world during my darkest moments.

Not with light that removed the darkness.

With presence that made the darkness navigable.

That is what I carried out of the desert.

Not the end of the dark.

The knowledge of what to look for when the dark arrives.

And it will arrive.

For every man who reads this.

Look up.

It is there.

It has always been there.

PART VI: COLLISION

CHAPTER 29

The Accident

The war ended in the desert.

But the desert did not end when the war did.

I returned to Las Pulgas on April 8, 1991. Walked across the parade deck alone while everyone else disappeared into arms that had been waiting. Picked up my bags. Walked back to the barracks. That was my welcome home. I carried my own bag. No one offered to help. That was the reality. Not the idea of family. Not the idea of welcome. The reality.

I had always carried my own bag.

Even as the youngest of eight in a house full of people on a sunny day, I had carried my own bag. The accident would later confirm what had always been true. That I moved through the most consequential moments of my life the same way I had arrived at everything else.

Alone.

The year between the desert and the collision was full.

Full in the way that false stability is always full. Moving fast enough that the thing underneath never had time to fully surface. The Corps had sent me back into the rhythm of service. Formations. Kitchens. Standards. The forward momentum of institutional life that does not pause for the particular kind of internal reckoning that the thin pamphlet and the handshake had told me to defer indefinitely.

I deferred it.

Not out of weakness. Out of the same discipline that had always carried me through. If endurance had worked in the desert it would work here. If control had held through the alarms and the food runs and the seven-second margins it would hold through this. If the container was strong enough to survive the war it was strong enough to survive the return.

That belief was both true and dangerous.

True because the container did hold. For a year it held. The functioning continued. The output met the standard. The external measures of discipline confirmed what the internal reality had quietly stopped confirming.

Dangerous because the container was not designed for permanent load-bearing. It was designed for emergency. For the duration of the crisis. For the interval between the alarm and the all-clear. And the all-clear had sounded. But I had not stood down.

The release valve opened slowly.

Alcohol was not a collapse. That is important to understand because collapse would have been visible and visible would have produced interruption. What alcohol was, in the year between the desert and the collision, was a quieting mechanism. A way to lower the volume on the thing that the combat had deposited in the body's account and that no amount of running or lifting or calling home from the payphone had fully addressed.

It worked.

That is the most dangerous thing about it.

It worked well enough that I did not recognize it as a problem. It worked well enough that the discipline and the function and the output continued alongside it. It worked well enough that the false stability remained stable. And the most dangerous moments are often the quietest ones. The ones that feel routine. Ordinary. Unremarkable.

July 8, 1992.

One year after the return. Still in the Marines. Still in uniform. Discharge date approaching. The life beyond the Corps beginning to take shape in the background.

The night started like any other.

Then everything changed.

Head-on collision.

The details of what the body went through in that moment are not the most important part of this chapter. But they are not nothing. They are the specific physical record of what impact at that level does to a human frame and they deserve to be stated plainly because plainness is the only language adequate to what happened.

I lost over three quarters of my blood.

I flatlined.

Momentarily. But completely. The monitors went flat. The room responded. And in the space between the flat line and the return, something happened that I will not reduce to metaphor or language that softens its meaning.

I had a conversation with God.

Five minutes. The number is specific because it was specific. Not a feeling of peace or a vague sense of light or any of the approximations that people use when they want to describe an encounter with something that language was not designed to contain. A conversation. Specific. Direct. Purposeful.

My mission was not done.

I was sent back.

That is the full statement of what was communicated. Not a command. Not a negotiation. A declaration. Your mission is not complete. Return and accomplish it.

I returned.

The body required specific and precise repair.

Crushed femur in multiple places. Fractured tailbone. The nose cut from my face by the hood of the car entering through the windshield. The edge of that hood carved upward through my face into my skull between my eyes. Glass shards embedded in my eyes and forehead.

Titanium rod installed down the center of the femur from knee to hip. Two screws on each end. The surgical team gave me the full accounting of what the repair required and what it could not guarantee. They told me I would never run again.

I noted that.

I did not accept it.

Thirteen days in the ICU. Twenty-one days in the hospital.

I did not call home.

I refused to let the military contact my family.

I refused a blood transfusion.

Those three decisions need to be understood together because they are the same decision expressed three times. I carry my own bag. I had always carried my own bag. The same man who walked alone across the parade deck on April 8, 1991 was the same man who lay in the ICU for thirteen days and chose to carry this alone as well. Not because he did not need support. Because support had never been offered at the moments that mattered. Not on the parade deck. Not when the list shrank to one name. Not in the desert with the thin pamphlet and the handshake.

I had learned not to expect it.

So I did not ask for it.

My family to this day do not fully remember the accident because they were not part of the experience. That is the reality. Not the idea of family. The reality of family. There is a difference. The idea of family is the version that shows up at the parade deck and holds the sign and absorbs the returning Marine into arms that have been waiting. The reality of family is the version that I had lived since I was the youngest of eight on a sunny day playing alone while eight people occupied the same house.

I went through it alone.

Same as the parade deck.

Same as always.

Three days in a coma while the conversation with God resolved itself into the clarity of a man who had been sent back with a purpose and a timeline and the specific understanding that the time he had been given was not incidental. It was assigned. And how he used it was the mission.

I carry my own bag.

But the bag had a destination now.

When I came out of the coma the doctors confirmed what the physical evidence had already stated. The injury was severe. The recovery would be long. The titanium rod was permanent. The prognosis for running was poor.

I heard all of that.

I noted it.

The body began its work.

Thirteen days in the ICU. The machines. The tubes. The particular quality of institutional silence that exists in a ward where everyone is fighting something that has not yet been decided. I was not afraid in that silence. The fear that had been present on the plane to the desert had let go years ago. What remained was the same thing that had remained after every difficult thing before this.

Presence.

The decision to be present in whatever the moment required.

The medical hold that followed lasted eighteen months.

Eighteen months of recovery. Of learning what the body could do and could not do and what the difference between could not and not yet actually was. Of running again. Not because the doctors said it was possible. Because I had been sent back with a mission and the mission required that the body be functional.

I ran.

Not immediately. Not without cost. But I ran.

Impact strips stories down to truth.

That line from the CANON source is the full summary of what the accident did to the false stability that had been operating as if it were genuine. The illusion that control was the same as healing. That discipline was the same as integration. That the container was infinite in its capacity.

The accident did not destroy me.

It interrupted momentum long enough for choice to return.

The conversation with God had made the destination clear.

Now came the work of becoming equal to it.

CHAPTER 30

Level Three

Level Three was not about alcohol.

That surprised me.

When I entered the program, I assumed the objective was obvious. Stop drinking. Manage triggers. Prevent relapse. That is surface work. Necessary, but surface. The kind of work that addresses the symptom while the source remains unnamed and intact and continuing to generate symptoms faster than the surface work can address them.

I had done surface work before.

I was good at surface work.

Surface work was the discipline of the preceding years. The control that held everything in place. The container that redistributed pressure without discharging it. The functioning that looked like mastery from the outside while something unnamed accumulated quietly on the inside. I had been doing surface work since the desert. Since the parade deck. Since the years of running three times a day and lifting heavy iron and calling home from the payphone and telling my mother I had returned physically but not spiritually.

Surface work was what I knew.

Level Three was excavation.

The first days were clinical. Assessments. Evaluations. Group sessions. Personal inventories. You begin by listing behaviors. How much. How often. Why.

But why is rarely honest at first.

I said I drank because of stress. Because of war. Because of pressure.

Those answers were accurate.

They were not complete.

Then the room changed.

Not the physical room. The emotional temperature of it. We were a group of Marines in that program. Different units. Different ranks. Different timelines. Different specific experiences of the war and the return and the years between. We did not know each other's full stories in the early days. We knew each other the way Marines know each other in a new environment. By posture. By what the body communicates before the mouth does. By the particular quality of contained pressure that every man in that room was carrying in his own specific form.

Then Desert Storm was brought up.

Nothing dramatic preceded it. No formal exercise. No therapist announcing that what was about to happen was significant. Just the name. The words. The particular combination of those two words that every man in that room had his own private relationship with.

Desert Storm.

Nothing was said.

Nothing needed to be said.

Uncontrollable tears.

Not from one man. From all of us.

The tears were not the same tears. What each man was releasing was his own. His specific account of what the war had placed in the body and what he had been carrying since and what the name Desert Storm unlocked in him when it was spoken in a room where the pretending was no longer available. But the release was simultaneous. Uncoordinated. Unplanned.

We all had demons inside from the war.

We had all been pretending.

To everyone else. And sometimes to ourselves.

That moment in the group room was the first time since the desert that I was in the company of people who did not require the pretending. Not because they asked me to stop. Because they had stopped themselves. Because the name of the war had stripped the surface away from all of us at once and what was underneath was not shame or weakness or the failure of the discipline we had been trained to maintain.

It was grief.

Unprocessed. Unnamed. Patient.

The grief of men who had been handed a thin pamphlet and a handshake and told to forget what happened and move on. Who had moved on. Who had applied every tool available to the project of moving on. And who had nonetheless arrived in a rehabilitation program eighteen months or two years or however many years after the desert because the moving on had been built on a foundation that the moving on itself had never addressed.

We wept together.

Without explanation.

Without anyone needing to ask what the other was carrying.

Because we already knew.

That moment was more therapeutic than any session that preceded it. Not because of what the therapist did. Because of what the room did. Because of the particular healing that is available only when you are in the company of people who share the weight you have been carrying alone and whose tears confirm that the weight was real and the carrying of it was not weakness but the only option the environment had ever offered.

The individual work continued alongside the group work.

Rehab removes distraction.

That is the most important thing to understand about what Level Three actually does before any clinical description makes sense. It removes distraction. The routines and the movement and the work and the particular forward momentum that had organized every day of my life since the first watch in the dark were not available here. There was no kitchen to run. No standard to hold for sixteen Marines. No mission that required the full deployment of attention and left no bandwidth for the thing underneath.

Here there was only the thing underneath.

We moved into regressive hypnosis.

I want to describe this carefully because the word hypnosis carries associations that do not fit what the experience actually was. This was not performance. Not suggestion. Not the kind of constructed unreality the word conjures. It was more like being guided into a particular quality of stillness deep enough that the defenses which ordinarily manage what the mind allows itself to access were no longer fully engaged.

What was accessed was not fabricated.

It was stored.

I remember the hallway.

Long. Dim. Quiet.

The quiet of a place that has been sealed for a long time. Not the watchful quiet of the watch that was full of presence and attention. The quiet of something that has not been visited. That has been holding what it holds without anyone coming to receive it.

Each number on the doors represented my age. Each door represented a year.

I moved through them.

Twenty. Nineteen. Eighteen.

Seventeen. Sixteen. Fifteen.

Fourteen. Thirteen. Twelve.

Ten. Nine. Eight.

Seven.

Six.

I stopped at six.

Not because I decided to stop. Because stopping was what the hallway required at that door. Because something in the body, below the level of conscious choice, recognized that what was behind door six was what the question had been pointing toward since the therapist first asked: when did you first learn to be alone?

I opened the door.

I was outside our old house.

It was a sunny day.

Beautiful sunlight warming my face. The kind of light that a child registers as the world being fundamentally generous, as the environment confirming that to exist in it is a good thing.

I was the youngest of eight.

Eight children in a house means the house is full. Means there is always someone present. Means that the physical conditions of solitude are almost never available.

Technically, never alone.

But inside, something was different.

I saw myself playing alone. Creating games alone. Laughing alone. Not because no one was there. Because something was present in me that was not present in the interaction with the people around me. A part of myself that had learned, at six years old, that the most essential version of who I was did not fully enter the shared space. That it stayed back. Watched. Created its own world within the larger world because the larger world did not have a container for it.

I had created joy because I felt alone even in a crowd.

That realization changed everything.

Alcohol had not created my isolation.

It had managed it.

That distinction is exact and it is the most important distinction in the chapter. I had not started drinking because I became isolated. I had been isolated since I was six years old, in a house full of people, on a sunny day. The alcohol arrived decades later and found that isolation already fully established and offered itself as a management tool.

Without alcohol, I felt that six-year-old again.

Level Three forced me to sit with him.

Not fix him. Not shame him. Understand him.

He was not the problem.

He was the source.

The source of the interior life that the watch had built on. That the kitchen had given shape to. That the desert had refined. That Orion had anchored. The six-year-old who played alone was the beginning of the man who could stand a four-hour watch in the dark without losing focus. The same solitude that had felt like isolation was the foundation of every quality that had followed.

I had never understood that until this room.

The six fragments of myself came into view.

The six-year-old. The Marine. The man who flatlined in the ICU with a crushed femur and a face rebuilt by surgeons and three days of conversation with God. The Corporal who earned the promotion because sobriety made him steady when others were not. The one in confinement who walked back into the unit without apology and rebuilt credibility through consistency alone. The man standing in the hallway opening the door at six.

No longer fragments.

One.

Solitude can be strength.

But secrecy becomes shame.

Shame is the silent accelerant of destruction.

I had been keeping the six-year-old secret. Not out of strategy. Out of the same instinct that had organized everything else. The belief that what was held inside was safer than what was released. Level Three showed me that belief had a limit. And I had reached it.

Level Three took three months.

When I walked out, the clarity that arrived was not the clarity of a problem solved. It was the clarity of a man who understood the full picture of where he had come from and what he was carrying and why he was carrying it and what he intended to do with the time he had been sent back to spend.

Clarity is prosperity.

Not the prosperity of accumulation. The prosperity of internal alignment. Of a person whose inside and outside are no longer operating on separate tracks.

I returned to my unit.

And something had shifted that did not shift back.

Passion for cooking and service did not arrive as new information. It arrived as recognition. As the thing I had always known meeting the clarity that Level Three had produced. The kitchen was not just where the pressure went. It was where I was meant to be. The work of feeding people, of holding the standard, of building teams and cultures around excellence, was not the management of the war's aftermath.

It was the mission.

The mission the conversation with God had sent me back to accomplish.

Focus blossomed.

Leadership honed.

This was when Master Sergeant Overton's leadership made its deepest impact. Not because Overton was new. Because I was new. The man who stood in front of him after Level Three was not the same man who had been running the kitchen before the accident. That man had been holding the standard through discipline. This man was holding it through understanding. The difference between those two things is everything.

This was when the Chief Cook billet was filled with everything it deserved.

This was when I became a public speaker.

Not by assignment. By invitation. The Marines who ran the program recognized that I had something specific to offer. Not the polished story of a man who had never struggled. The living example of a man who had struggled, who had gone through Level Three, who had sat in the room and wept with other veterans when Desert Storm was named, and who had come out the other side with something real to say about what was inside and what it cost to leave it unaddressed.

I spoke at parades.

To thousands of Marines.

About alcohol. About war. About the distance between the mission and the man. About what happens when you pretend to be okay for long enough that the pretending becomes indistinguishable from being okay. About the room where Desert Storm was named and no one needed to say anything because the tears said everything.

I used my mistake as an example.

Not as confession or self-punishment or the performance of accountability for an audience. As a living example. As the specific and honest account of a man whose Creator gave him more time and who chose to use that time to benefit the people who had a listening for him.

Who walked the walk with him.

Who didn't leave him to play by himself.

And that mattered more than anything.

Who actually has a listening for your greatness.

Find that listening.

Be thankful for your time.

Make a difference.

Deal in reality versus illusion no matter where it takes you.

From that point forward, my life would not be driven by reaction.

It would be driven by integration.

Integration is mastery.

Not the mastery of control. Not the mastery of the standard held without apology. The mastery of a person who has understood the full picture of who they are and has chosen, consciously and with full awareness, how to carry it forward.

The watch had built presence. The kitchen had built precision. The desert had built endurance. Orion had built orientation. Level Three built integration.

And integration is where mastery begins.

Not in the discipline that holds things in place.

In the understanding of what needs to be held.

And what needs to be released.

PART VII: RETURN

CHAPTER 31

Back to Pulgas

Redemption does not arrive with noise.

It does not come with ceremony. It does not announce itself or demand acknowledgment or require the people around you to pause and mark the moment when the version of yourself that came through the accident and the ICU and the court- martial and Level Three walks back through the door.

It comes in routine.

Morning. Formation. Work. Responsibility.

I came back to the same place.

Las Pulgas. The same base. The same buildings. The same hierarchy and the same institutional rhythms and the same Marines who had been there when I left and who had watched what happened and who had formed their own assessments of what I was and what I had done and what I was likely to be going forward.

But I wasn't the same.

That asymmetry is the full statement of where I stood when I walked back through that door. The place had not changed. I had. And the work of Part VII is not the drama of announcement or the performance of transformation. It is the quiet daily proof that the change was real.

There is a difference between surviving consequence and integrating it.

Survival is passive. Survival says I made it through. Integration is active. Integration says I am different now.

The Marine Corps does not reward speeches. It rewards steadiness. I did not over-explain what had happened. I did not perform humility. I did not attempt to rewrite the narrative into something more palatable or more heroic or more aligned with how I wanted to be seen.

I worked.

I showed up early.

I followed through.

I responded calmly when the situation wanted me to react.

I did not drink.

I did not posture.

I did not avoid eye contact.

Consistency is how credibility returns. Not instantly. Gradually. Through the accumulation of days where the behavior confirms what the mouth has claimed. Through the particular proof that only time produces. You cannot counterfeit restraint. You cannot counterfeit internal discipline. You cannot counterfeit ownership. These things show themselves or they don't and there is nothing else available to substitute for them.

Marines observe quietly.

They watch posture. They watch tone. They watch reaction under pressure. Before the accident I had understood discipline as external compliance. Follow orders. Meet the standard. Produce the output. After the accident, after the ICU and the three days in a coma and the five-minute conversation with God and the hallway and the door at six, discipline had become something else entirely.

Internal architecture.

External discipline says follow orders.

Internal discipline says govern yourself.

That shift changes everything.

The standard was still there.

Now I understood it differently. Clearer. Sharper.

The standard before Level Three had been Overton's standard, which was the finest standard available and which I had carried with genuine pride and genuine commitment. But I had been carrying it through discipline. Through the external imposition of a requirement that I had internalized deeply enough to hold without being told. That is real and it is valuable and it is not nothing.

After Level Three I was carrying it through understanding.

Not the understanding of technique or of the operational requirement. The understanding of why it mattered. Not because Overton had said it should. Not because the best mess hall on Camp Pendleton was a worthy aspiration. Because the work of feeding people, of holding the standard, of building something excellent out of the materials available, was connected to the mission the conversation with God had sent me back to accomplish.

That mission had a name now.

Not a title or a position or a formal designation.

A direction.

Use the time. Make a difference. Use the voice to benefit the people who have a listening for you.

The promotion to Corporal came during this season.

Not because I had survived. Not because I had suffered. Not because the institution felt pity for a man who had flatlined in an ICU and lost three quarters of his blood and been given back by God and then walked through a court-martial and thirty days of confinement and three months of Level Three.

Because I was steady.

Steadiness is the most reliable signal of genuine change. Anyone can perform recovery. Anyone can demonstrate the visible markers of improvement under observation and revert to the original pattern when the observation ends. Steadiness is different. Steadiness is what happens when the change has gone deep enough that it no longer requires effort to maintain. When the governing of yourself has become structural rather than aspirational.

I became steady.

Younger Marines began approaching me quietly.

Not because I was perfect. Because I had failed publicly and recovered visibly. That combination is rare and it produces a specific kind of authority that perfection cannot generate. The Marines who came to me had not failed in the way I had failed. But they were carrying things. Pressure from the war. Questions they did not have language for. The particular weight of men who had been trained to move forward without looking at what the moving forward was leaving behind.

They asked about drinking. About anger. About pressure.

I spoke plainly.

War changes you. Pretending it doesn't is dangerous. But your behavior afterward is still your responsibility. Explanation without ownership becomes excuse. Ownership without understanding becomes shame. You need both.

They listened because they had seen the court-martial. They had seen the confinement. They had seen me return steady. Redemption becomes credible when it costs something. Mine had cost pride and comfort and reputation. But it had given back something that none of those things could purchase.

Self-respect.

Self-respect is quiet alignment between action and belief.

When you can look at yourself honestly and not flinch, something stabilizes. I no longer needed approval. I no longer needed to prove toughness. I no longer needed to dominate rooms. Redemption removes the need to perform. It leaves presence.

Presence under pressure becomes leadership.

Leadership without rank is the purest kind.

Then they asked me to speak publicly.

Not to one Marine or a small group in a quiet corridor. At parades. In front of thousands.

I stood in front of Marines who were where I had been. Not identical situations but identical architecture. The pressure that has nowhere to go. The pretending that calcifies over time into something indistinguishable from being okay. The questions that do not get asked because the culture that produced them has no container for the asking.

I spoke from what I had lived.

Not from what I had studied or been trained to say or been given by an institution that had handed out a thin pamphlet and called it sufficient. From the ICU and the hallway and the door at six and the desert and the parade deck and every moment of carrying my own bag through things that the people standing in front of me had also been carrying.

I used my mistake as an example.

My Creator gave me more time. I chose to use that time to make a difference in the lives of people who had a listening for what I had become.

Then came the skydive.

Not random. Not reckless. The specific and deliberate answer to a question that the steadiness had produced.

I had been resuscitated. I had been reconstructed. I had walked back into my unit after confinement and earned back what needed to be earned back. I had stood in front of thousands of Marines and spoken plainly about the war and the pressure and what it cost to leave it unaddressed. All of that had confirmed what Level Three had built.

But a quiet question remained.

Am I still alive? Not biologically. Viscerally.

Desert Storm had imprinted intensity into my nervous system. The desert sky and Orion overhead and the seven-second margins and the food runs through destruction. After the accident, after being given back, stability had arrived. Clarity. Steadiness. All of it was real and all of it was necessary.

But after intensity, stability can feel muted.

I did not want chaos.

But I needed to know something.

Could I still walk the line consciously?

It was my twenty-third birthday.

I chose skydiving as a gift to myself. Not a party. Not alcohol. Not noise. A jump.

Thirteen thousand feet.

At least fifteen Marines said they would go. The talk was loud. The energy confident. As the day approached the numbers thinned. Excuses surfaced. Nerves disguised as logistics.

By the morning of the jump I was alone.

I drove myself.

There is a pattern in my life of crossing thresholds alone. Returning from war alone. Facing ICU alone. Representing myself in court alone. Refusing the blood transfusion alone. Now this.

The airfield was quiet. Cold wind across open land. The hum of engines warming. I signed the waiver.

You may die.

I had already signed that document in other forms.

The instructor strapped himself to my back. We climbed. At altitude the door opened. Cold air struck like a wall. The earth looked small.

There is a literal line at the edge of that door.

One foot inside. One foot out.

War had forced me across a line. The accident had thrown me across it. Resuscitation had pulled me back.

This time I stepped.

Freefall is clarity.

Wind against the face. Time stretching. No narrative. No history. No shame.

Only now.

I felt alive.

Not reckless. Not destructive.

Present.

The parachute opened. Silence replaced the rush. Floating replaced falling.

Hanging under canopy I understood something important.

Nothing will ever feel like Desert Storm again.

And it shouldn't.

War is imposed intensity. This was chosen.

That difference is maturity.

When my boots touched the ground I stood still.

Ground under my feet. Second chance validated.

Celebration of survival. Celebration of sobriety. Celebration of promotion. Celebration of being given back.

After that jump every step felt different.

I did not need chaos to feel alive.

I could choose intensity without destruction.

I was not broken. I was not numb. I was not drifting.

I was integrated.

The uniform would come off soon.

But when it did I would leave anchored.

Because I had already crossed the line.

On purpose.

And that changed everything about what came next.

CHAPTER 32

The Sound Changed

Sound had been changing for a long time before I understood what it was changing into.

Chapter 14 had described it. The ports of the Pacific. The Philippines. Malaysia. The nights in the streets of places that did not organize themselves around the rhythms I had grown up with. Music drifting from windows and doorways. Beats built on repetition instead of melody. Patterns that looped and layered rather than resolving toward a conclusion. I had not known the names for any of it. But something in the structure had lodged itself.

The repetition was not boring.

It was stabilizing.

A steady pulse you could orient to when everything else felt unanchored. Pattern without explanation. Presence without destination. The music that did not demand emotion or tell a story or offer a resolution. It simply existed. Consistent. Unbothered by interpretation. Moving forward through its own logic without asking whether the person listening was ready.

I had understood that quality intuitively on the Pacific without having language for why it felt right. The same way I had looked at Orion before I had a name for it and had felt the reliance before I had the framework.

The body knows what the mind has not yet organized.

Before we deployed, music was shifting.

The late eighties and the turn into the nineties. The radio and the culture and the particular sound of a country processing things it did not have direct language for either. Transition in the air. The old structures loosening. Something rawer beginning to emerge from underneath the polished surface of what popular music had been.

We left before it fully arrived.

When we came back, it had arrived.

Nirvana. Soundgarden. Alice in Chains.

Raw. Unfiltered.

It matched what we carried inside.

That sentence requires full examination because it is the most precise description of what the sound change actually meant. Not that the music was good or that it was culturally significant or that it represented a generational shift in American popular culture. All of those things were true and none of them is the point. The point is that it matched. The point is that for the first time since before the desert, the sound coming out of speakers and radios and cassette players was organized around an interior reality that resembled the one I was living in.

Grunge did not resolve.

That is the essential quality. The house music on the Pacific had not resolved either. It had pressed forward without arriving anywhere. It had existed in its own present tense. Grunge was the American version of the same principle. It did not build toward release in the way that the music of the preceding decades had built toward release. It stayed in its own weight. It sat with its own darkness rather than offering a way out of it.

A generation of young people who had grown up during the Cold War, who had watched the world hold itself at the edge of catastrophe for decades, had produced music that sounded like what it felt like to grow up inside that tension. And a group of Marines who had just come back from a war that the country had already moved past without pausing to acknowledge what it had done to the people it sent, found that sound and recognized something in it.

This is what we carried.

Not in those words. We did not have those words. We did not sit in circles and analyze the sociological function of Kurt Cobain or the cultural significance of grunge as the sound of unprocessed collective trauma. We just turned it up.

Because it sounded like what was inside.

Intensity without resolution. Pressure without the guarantee of relief. The acknowledgment that something difficult was present and that the appropriate response to its presence was not to smooth it over with production values but to stay inside it and let it exist in its full unresolved weight.

That matched.

Before the return, I had been trying to manage what was inside by building a container strong enough to hold it. Level Three had changed the relationship. The container was not the goal. Understanding what was in the container was the goal. And once you understood it, the containing became less urgent because the thing being contained was no longer an unnamed threat.

The sound changed because I changed.

Not that Nirvana sounded different to me than it sounded to someone who had not been to the desert. That what I brought to the listening was different. The ears that received it had been through things that the music, without knowing anything about me, had somehow accounted for. Had stayed in the weight of. Had refused to resolve prematurely.

I needed music that would stay in the weight with me.

Soundgarden stayed. Alice in Chains stayed. The particular distorted texture of guitars run through amplifiers with too much gain, the vocals that did not ask for your sympathy but simply stated what they were carrying, the drumming that hit like something with mass and intention.

It all matched.

Not as escape.

As recognition.

There is a difference between music that takes you out of where you are and music that confirms where you are. The house music on the Pacific had been stabilizing, a pattern you could hold onto when everything else was unanchored. The grunge was different. It was not asking to stabilize anything. It was asking to be honest about what was there.

And honesty, after the years of containment and the accident and the ICU and the court-martial and Level Three and the hallway and the door at six, was the specific thing I had been building capacity for.

The music met me in that capacity.

The sound had changed.

And in changing, it had confirmed something that the skydive had also confirmed. That the work had landed. That the man who stood with one foot inside and one foot outside the door of a plane at thirteen thousand feet and stepped into freefall by choice was not the same man who had boarded the plane to the desert with twenty-two hours of fear.

That man had been moving toward something he could not name.

This man knew what he was moving toward.

Use the time.

Make a difference.

Deal in reality versus illusion no matter where it takes you.

The music that stayed in its own weight rather than resolving prematurely was not pessimistic. It was honest about the cost of existence. And honesty about the cost was the beginning of clarity about the value.

You cannot fully appreciate what you have been given back if you have not fully acknowledged what the having of it required.

The sound acknowledged that.

So did I.

The uniform was coming off soon.

The institutional structure that had organized every morning since the first day of service was going to stop organizing mornings. The formation, the standard, the particular daily architecture of military life that had been both the container and the content of who I was for five and a half years, was preparing to release me into something it had not designed me for.

Civilian life.

The sound was going to have to come with me.

Not the specific music. The quality of it. The willingness to stay in the weight rather than resolving prematurely. The recognition that unresolved does not mean unfinished. That some things are not meant to resolve into relief but are meant to be lived inside of with full presence and full acknowledgment and the particular kind of steadiness that comes not from the absence of weight but from having learned to carry it with intention.

That is what the sound change confirmed.

That I could carry what I was carrying.

Not perfectly. Not without cost.

With intention.

And that was enough to take the next step.

CHAPTER 33

The Long Way Home

November 18, 1993.

The uniform came off.

Five and a half years of structure folded into a garment bag and placed in the back of a closet. Desert Storm. ICU. Court-martial. Level Three. Promotion to Corporal. Public speaking to thousands. Skydiving at thirteen thousand feet on my twenty-third birthday.

Honorable discharge.

The Last Formation was not dramatic. It did not need to be. It was the closing of a chapter written in heat. I stood there with the knowledge of what I had survived and the knowledge of what I had chosen. I had been shown what I was capable of. I had been given a second chance. I had been offered a path of destruction and refused it. I had been tempted to live numb and chose clarity instead.

When the paperwork was final and the uniform was no longer mine to wear, I did not feel like the fire went out.

It didn't.

Discharge papers do not discharge the nervous system.

That is the first thing to understand about what it means to walk out of five and a half years of military service and into a world that has not been organized around the same requirements. The structure stops. The institution releases you. The daily architecture of formations and standards and the particular rhythm of institutional life that has been defining every morning since the first day of service simply ends.

And what you discover is that the structure was never only external.

It had become internal long ago.

I came home.

Back to Saint Louis. Back to the house that had built me. The same house where I once stood in sunlight at six years old feeling both loved and alone. The same yard. The same Midwest winter air cutting through the same sky.

Only now I carried something different inside me.

No firearm. That chapter was closed.

But knives. Yes.

Blades were constant. In my pocket. In my truck. In my bag. Not because I was looking for violence. Because preparedness had become muscle memory. A man who has lived in sustained threat does not immediately walk unarmed through a world that pretends threat does not exist. The body had been trained for too long to interpret the absence of a weapon as vulnerability. The knives were not aggression.

Thcy were continuity.

Steel-toe civilian boots replaced combat boots. I chose them deliberately. The weight grounded me. The firmness reminded me I was still responsible for my footing even when the ground had stopped moving like desert sand or a flat-bottomed ship in the Pacific.

When I entered restaurants, I instinctively chose seats with my back to the wall. I scanned exits without thinking. I tracked hands when doors opened. I noted who was agitated, who was distracted, who was present.

Hypervigilance is not drama.

It is wiring.

And mine was wired.

But not all of me came back.

That took time. Years. And the man who went in was not the man who came out. And the one who came out was still becoming.

For six months I drew unemployment. I stayed in the house I grew up in. I watched my nieces and nephews while my sister finished school.

Some would see unemployment as drift.

It wasn't.

It was decompression.

Five and a half years of intensity does not unwind overnight. If you rush into noise, you carry combat tempo into civilian chaos. The machine does not know how to downshift when the only speeds it has known are forward and faster. I refused to rush. I chose decompression the way I had chosen the skydive.

Deliberately.

Consciously.

Children slowed me.

They did not care about rank. They did not care about medals or court-martial or sobriety milestones or the titanium rod in my femur or the groove in my skull between my eyes. They cared if I would sit on the floor and build blocks. If I would chase them in the yard. If I would listen.

Children live in present tense.

They do not scan exits. They do not carry knives. They do not measure threat in every room. They simply exist in the moment they are in with the full unselfconscious presence of people who have not yet been taught to be anywhere other than exactly where they are.

That slowed my nervous system in ways nothing else could.

I would wake before sunrise out of habit. Sit in the living room in silence while the house slept. No formation. No command. Just breath. At first silence felt foreign. The kind of silence that happens when the institutional noise that has been organizing your perception for years suddenly stops and the absence of it feels louder than the thing itself.

Then it felt earned.

But something else was happening at night.

The dreams returned.

Snakes.

Not random. Not occasional. Repeated.

Coiling. Watching. Silent. Patient. Sometimes striking. Sometimes simply existing. Night after night.

I would wake alert, heart elevated, body ready.

Most people suppress recurring dreams. They manage them the way I had always managed the things I did not want to fully address. Through the forward motion of the day. Through the discipline of not stopping long enough to let the unnamed thing surface.

Level Three had shown me that management without examination was exactly the pattern that had built the pressure to the point of the accident.

I was not going to repeat it.

I confronted the dream.

If my subconscious was surfacing snakes I would not hide from them. I would study them.

So I bought one.

A Colombian red-tail boa.

A baby. Small enough to wrap easily around my forearm. Strong enough to command respect. Calm enough to reveal something deeper than fear.

When I brought it home people assumed I was trying to prove something.

I wasn't.

I was integrating something.

Fear loses power when examined directly.

The first time I wrapped that boa around my neck something shifted. Cold scales. Slow muscle movement. Steady breath. No panic. No aggression.

Presence.

Snakes conserve energy. They do not waste motion. They strike only when necessary. They rest without apology. They exist in their own nature without performing anything for anyone watching.

There was grounding in that.

I began walking around Saint Louis with that snake around my neck. People stared. Some stepped away. Some laughed. Some shook their heads. It didn't matter.

It wasn't performance.

It was confrontation.

If fear lives in shadow, bring it into daylight. Look at it directly. Wrap it around your neck and walk through the world with it visible and discover that the thing you were afraid of cannot survive your full undivided attention.

During that same season I was deep into Rasta philosophy.

Grounded. Peaceful. Raw truth.

Rasta stripped away noise. Live naturally. Respect life. Reject systems that consume without awareness. Speak truth without aggression. See through the constructed reality that institutions and cultures and the particular social agreements of any given moment present as permanent and find what is actually true underneath.

After war, that resonated. After court-martial, that resonated. After rehab, that resonated.

Rasta grounded the intensity inside me without dulling it. It did not ask me to become less than what I was. It asked me to be more intentional about what I was aimed at.

Deal in reality versus illusion no matter where it takes you.

The nightmares began to lessen.

Not because I eliminated them. Because I integrated them. The snake in my hands and the snake in my dreams were the same message. Look directly. Do not manage. Confront.

Knives remained. Steel-toe boots remained. Exit scanning remained. The wiring did not disappear because I sat with a boa and studied Rasta philosophy in Saint Louis. That was never the goal. The goal was what Chapter 30 had named.

Integration is mastery.

Not the elimination of what the war built. The reclamation of it. The deliberate choice of what to do with what had been installed. The knives that had been muscle memory became instruments of nourishment in a different way. The precision that had cooked 2,880 strips of bacon across sixteen ovens without burning one was the same precision that would define a culinary career. The hypervigilance that had kept me alive in the desert became the awareness that makes a great chef see the whole kitchen simultaneously.

Nothing was wasted.

Everything was redirected.

January 1994 came.

Culinary school began.

Chef coats replaced camouflage. Knives became instruments of nourishment. Heat returned but creative heat. The Marine in me translated seamlessly.

Show up early. Keep your station clean. Respect hierarchy. Communicate clearly. Execute precisely.

But kitchens introduced something the Corps never required.

Creativity.

In the Marines, innovation under pressure can cost lives. In a kitchen, innovation builds flavor. Fire can destroy. Or fire can nourish. That distinction shifted something deep inside me. The fire did not go out when the uniform came off. It changed fuel. It stopped being a wildfire and became a furnace. Directional. Purposeful. Heat that forged rather than heat that consumed.

Forged in heat.

Not a metaphor. A description.

Everything I had been through since the first night in the desert looking up at a pattern, I did not yet have a name for had been forging something. The watch and the kitchen and the standard and the parade deck and the plane and the beast released and the war and the accident and the conversation with God and the hallway and the door at six and the steadiness and the skydive and the boa and the children living in present tense.

All of it had been the heat.

The furnace producing something that civilian life and culinary school and everything that followed would have a chance to use.

I walked away from the Corps not cured, not finished, not neatly resolved. But integrated. Disciplined. Alert. Alive.

The world beyond the gate was less structured. More ambiguous. More tempting. But I was not walking into it empty.

You will meet yourself face to face in the darkness and discover what you are truly made of.

I had met myself.

In the desert. In the ICU. In the hallway with the numbered doors. On the parade deck on April 8, 1991. In the group room when Desert Storm was named and no one needed to say anything because the tears said everything.

I had met myself and I had not looked away.

That was the full education.

Not the kitchen. Not the war. Not the accident.

The willingness to look directly at what was there and to stay in the looking until the understanding arrived.

The house that once held a six-year-old boy who felt alone now held a man who had crossed death's threshold and returned with a mission. The yard was the same. The Midwest winter air was the same. The sky was the same sky that had been above the Pacific and above the desert and above the parade deck.

And somewhere in it, Orion.

Fixed. Present. Unmoved by everything that had happened beneath it.

Still there.

The pack never comes off.

What changes is whether it's still doing the walking.

I stepped into civilian air for the last time as a Marine.

I was still walking.

Not because the weight was gone.

Because I had finally understood what I was carrying.

And where it was meant to go.

EPILOGUE

Contained Fire

I did not leave the Marine Corps the way I entered it.

I entered as a boy with raw ambition and a hunger for structure I could not name yet. I entered believing discipline was something you borrowed from an institution, a set of rules that would shape you if you stayed close enough to it. I entered thinking strength was volume, speed, and certainty.

But I did not leave that way.

I left with silence in my chest and steadiness in my hands. Quiet proof that discipline is not borrowed. It is built. It is carried. And if you do the work, it becomes yours.

The fire did not go out.

It changed fuel.

This is the full statement of what Book I has been.

Not a record of what happened to me. A reckoning with what it produced. The war and the kitchen and the standard and the parade deck and the accident and the coma and the court-martial and the hallway and the door at six and the skydive and the boa and the children living in present tense. All of it was heat. All of it was forging something. The question this book has been answering, from the first night in the desert lying in the sand looking up at a pattern I did not yet have a name for, is what the heat was making.

The answer is this:

A man who can hold intensity without being consumed by it.

A man who has met himself face to face in the darkness and discovered what he was truly made of.

A man who carries his own bag.

Not because no one offered.

Because carrying it was the work.

The months after war taught me that you can return physically and still not come home. April 8, 1991 was not a celebration for me. I returned to a parade deck full of families, arms open, banners raised, love waiting in the sunlight. And then there was my empty space. No one there for me. I picked up my gear and walked back to the barracks alone.

That was the first lesson in the second war.

Not bullets.

Absence.

And absence does something to a man if he cannot name it. It creates pressure. It builds heat behind the ribs. It makes you look for a release valve, anything that will bleed it off long enough to sleep.

Alcohol became that valve for many of us. For too many.

I watched the aftermath unfold in stories first, then in names, then in people I had seen squared away before the desert ever touched them. Men who had been sane. Men who had laughed with us, trained with us, stood in formation looking like the kind of Marines you could trust in the dark. Then they went home and detonated.

It was an epidemic wearing camouflage.

And it terrified me. Not because I thought I was better than them. Because I knew the truth that no one wanted to say out loud.

A man is capable of more than he thinks.

That fear was part of why I did not go home immediately. My body was back but my spirit was still scanning the perimeter. I ran three times a day because movement made the pressure manageable. I lifted because weight felt like control. I stood at payphones calling my mother because her voice was one of the few things that could reach me across the distance between who I used to be and who I was becoming.

Then the accident happened and the fire roared.

I do not remember the crash the way I remember other things. I remember the consequence. I remember waking to a room full of doctors in the ICU, eight of them, standing there like witnesses. The words miracle and reconstruction and how did you survive this. The crushed femur. The choice between a titanium rod and amputation. The face split open by the hood of the car, the nose torn, the groove carved between my eyes like a river in bone that never fully disappeared.

I refused the blood transfusion.

I refused to contact family.

Not from cruelty.

From calibration.

I had already learned what absence looked like. I had already seen what it meant to return and have no one waiting. And in that ICU bed I made a decision that was both faith and truth. If I was supposed to be here I would be here. If I wasn't, then I would meet God clean.

I went into a coma for three days.

And in my memory, it was not three days.

It was a conversation.

A brief exchange with the Creator.

Not bargaining. Not panic. Not pleading. Just presence.

And the message was simple: you are not finished.

When I came back, I did not come back the same. Death does not leave you untouched. The boundary between here and there changes a man's relationship with time. You stop treating hours like a guaranteed supply. You stop assuming there will be another season to get things right. You start hearing decisions differently, like doors closing or opening, not like ideas floating in air.

The court-martial came next and it was clear the institution wanted a story.

A cautionary tale.

An example.

They wanted to burn me and let the smoke warn everyone else.

But by then the pieces on the chessboard were already moving and I had already learned to see the game.

I represented myself.

No jury.

Judge alone.

I watched the pressure they put on the Marines from the other truck, men they wanted to persuade into testimony that would seal my fate.

But we ran deep. Too much history. Too many road trips. Too much brotherhood built in places outside the frame of official record.

When it came time to speak, they testified for me.

Not with emotion.

With truth.

They explained that I had already filed paperwork to pay for the truck immediately, that the unit kept denying processing, that I started paying cash before the trial even began.

Strategically, I could not be touched.

Most charges dropped.

What was sentenced felt like vacation compared to what they had intended. Thirty days solitary, interrupted twice a week for physical therapy on my broken femur.

And who picked me up for therapy?

My boys.

The same men they tried to turn against me.

That was not luck.

That was relationship.

That was consequence paying off in the only currency that matters in hard times: who will stand with you when it costs something.

Then Level Three happened.

Rehab was not humiliation.

It was excavation.

It did not just remove alcohol. It pulled the root out and held it in the light. It showed me that war did not invent my isolation. It amplified it. It showed me a hallway in my mind where each door was an age and it led me back to six years old. Sunlight on my skin. Happiness created by my own imagination. And sadness underneath because I felt alone even surrounded by people.

That discovery did not weaken me.

It explained me.

And explanation is power.

Sobriety grew into prosperity. Not money. Not comfort. Clarity. My mind became quieter. My reactions became cleaner. My discipline stopped being a performance and became a posture. That posture earned trust again. That trust brought promotion. Corporal was not handed to me as sympathy. It was earned as proof.

Then on my twenty-third birthday I did something that looked like adrenaline from the outside but was actually ceremony on the inside.

Skydiving.

Thirteen thousand feet.

Fifteen Marines said they would go, all confident until the date approached and people started backing out.

By the day of the jump, I drove myself.

Again.

There is a recurring pattern in my life where thresholds are crossed alone. Not because I wanted isolation. Because when the line appears, some men talk. Some men step.

I stepped.

Freefall was not chaos.

It was clarity.

Wind against my face. Time stretched thin. The ground far below. No narrative, no history, no court, no ICU, no shame.

Only now.

War is imposed intensity.

Skydiving was voluntary.

That distinction matters.

When my boots touched the ground, every step afterward felt different. Not because I was invincible. Because I was deliberate. I had walked the line again. I had crossed it by choice.

Nothing will ever feel like Desert Storm again.

And it shouldn't.

The goal is not to recreate war in civilian life. The goal is to take the discipline forged there and build something that does not destroy you.

Then came the white dog.

The dreams had been returning in the months after Level Three. Not the nightmares of Chapter 6, not the symbolic dreams of violation and defense. Something different.

I dreamed of a white dog.

In the dream it attacked. And in the dream, I responded out of protection. Not rage. Protection.

Months later, walking toward the chow hall, I saw a white dog in the same area as the dream. Highly unlikely on base. Uncommon enough that it stopped time for a second.

Not fear.

Recognition.

Recognition is different than fear.

Fear hijacks you.

Recognition observes.

My body registered the stimulus in a microsecond. The dream memory lit up like a match. The old wiring offered its old answer.

But I did not move toward violence.

I stayed composed.

I walked past it.

I did not need to kill what no longer threatened me.

I never saw that dog again.

It was not supernatural. It was surreal. Like the mind testing whether the work held. Like life placing a mirror in front of me and asking a question without words.

Are you still reactive?

Or are you restrained?

That moment mattered more than I admitted at the time. Because it proved something I needed proven. The dream had shown what I was capable of. Reality showed what I would choose.

The discipline had become restraint.

And restraint is the completion of the title of this book.

Discipline. Fire. Restraint.

Not discipline alone which can become rigidity. Not fire alone which becomes wildfire. Restraint. The container that makes discipline purposeful and fire productive. The understanding that power is not measured by what you release. It is measured by what you choose not to.

The fire did not go out.

It changed fuel.

It stopped being a wildfire.

It became a furnace.

Directional.

Purposeful.

Heat that forged rather than heat that consumed.

I walked away from the Corps not cured, not finished, not neatly resolved. But integrated. Disciplined. Alert. Alive. The world beyond the gate would not be easier. Less structured. More ambiguous. More tempting. But I was not walking into it empty.

And to whoever reads this and recognizes something in it, something in the pressure without a name, something in the carrying alone, something in the parade deck with no one waiting, something in the hallway with the numbered doors:

You will meet yourself face to face in the darkness.

And you will discover what you are truly made of.

Not in the comfortable moments. Not in the recognized ones. In the ones that strip everything away. In the desert and the ICU and the courtroom and the hallway and the door at six.

That is where you find out.

Find the people who have a listening for your greatness.

Not the people who celebrate your performance. The ones who stayed when staying cost something. The boys who drove me to physical therapy after a court-martial meant to break me. The nieces and nephews who did not care about rank and pulled me into present tense with their whole unburdened hearts. The Marines in the group room who wept when Desert Storm was named because they were carrying the same thing in different forms.

Find that listening.

Be thankful for your time.

Make a difference.

Deal in reality versus illusion no matter where it takes you.

The pack never comes off.

What changes is whether it's still doing the walking.

And as I stepped into civilian air for the last time as a Marine, I knew one thing with absolute certainty.

I was still walking.

Not because the weight was gone.

Because I understood what I was carrying.

And I knew where it was meant to go.

The military was not the story.

It was the foundation.

Every kitchen I would build. Every team I would lead. Every company I would name Orion. Every table I would set. Every life I would touch through food and service and the particular kind of leadership that is only available to a person who has been stripped down to nothing and chose to come back anyway.

None of it would exist without this.

Without the watch in the dark. Without the 2 a.m. kitchen. Without the sixteen ovens and the 2,880 strips of bacon. Without the parade deck and the plane and the beast released. Without the sand and the smoke and Orion overhead. Without the accident and the coma and the conversation with God. Without the hallway and the door at six.

Book, I end here.

But the story does not.

What the Marines forged in me became the fire that built a culinary career, an entrepreneurial life, and a mission that is still unfolding. The discipline installed in the desert became the foundation of everything extraordinary that followed.

Book II will show you what a man does with a second chance.

Book III will show you what a man becomes when he finally understands why he was sent back.

This is only the beginning.

Seek him that maketh the seven stars and Orion, and turneth the shadow of death into the morning, and maketh the day dark with night: that calleth for the waters of the sea, and poureth them out upon the face of the earth: The Lord is his name.

Amos 5:8